MW01076063

POACHER WARS

A PENNSYLVANIA GAME WARDEN'S JOURNAL

By

William Wasserman

Copyright © 2008 by Penn's Woods Publications

ISBN 0-9718907-6-5

Cover photo by John Wasserman

Also by William Wasserman

Game Warden
Wildlife Guardian
Trapping Secrets
Pennsylvania Wildlife Tails
More Pennsylvania Wildlife Tails

For my beloved children:
Jesse and Sarah

Introduction

As a Pennsylvania game warden for more than three decades, I patrolled four-hundred square miles of rugged mountain terrain where I pursued poachers on foot and by vehicle and boat. Along the way, I investigated thousands of game law violations and arrested many violent career poachers.

The hardcore poacher is not just some poor, down-on-his-luck rascal looking for meat to feed his hungry family. Many are serious outlaws with extensive criminal records. Throughout my career, I've encountered a number of poachers who were convicted felons, including murderers, drug addicts, dope dealers, and outlaw bikers. Herein, you will find sixteen true stories about some of these dangerous and unpredictable men.

The incidents recounted in this book are real; however, the stories are based on my memories over a period of years and may differ from the memories of others. I admit to taking some creative liberties with events and to re-creating some of the dialog. I have also given the poachers and their associates fictitious names and have altered their physical descriptions. Any resemblance to actual persons, living or dead is entirely coincidental.

Ned Viper

***THE PISTOL HAD BEEN** tucked in the small of his back all along, and when he began to draw I reached for my gun with fated dread . . .*

It was a hot, humid July day when the woman called about a raccoon cub that had bitten her daughter. Now it was mysteriously dead in its cage and her daughter sick. She asked me to come by and pick up the cub for a rabies examination, her voice edged with fear. I assured her I would. Pennsylvania had over six hundred rabies incidents that year, with raccoons accounting for two-thirds.

As I pulled into the narrow dirt driveway leading to her trailer, I came upon four makeshift doghouses surrounding the property like cruel sentry boxes, each housing a surly mongrel. They lunged at their chains, barking and snarling furiously as I parked my vehicle and walked through the baking midday sun to the front door.

I knocked and soon a burly woman appeared in a faded plaid shirt that fell loosely over tattered jeans. Two small girls clung to her shirttail and stared at me with dark apprehension. One had a freshly bandaged forearm. I smiled at them over the frenzied barking behind me.

"State game warden," I began. "I'm here about the raccoon"—

"SHUT UP!" the woman bellowed. And there was an abrupt sweet silence as the dogs scurried into their rude shelters. She eyed me critically for a moment, then pointed a stout finger past my shoulder. "It's buried back there. You'll see the fresh dirt."

"Has your daughter seen a doctor?"

"'Course she has! That's why *you're* here; he wants the critter tested."

"Would you mind stepping out to show me exactly where it's buried?"

Two fleshy arms pushed the girls firmly behind her. "You kids stay here," she scolded. Then she brushed by me and waddled across her parched lawn in soiled, bare feet. I turned and followed, her dogs snarling balefully as I passed, warning me not to come close.

Buried in a shallow depression, the cub had already begun to decay from the intense summer heat. I retrieved the carcass with gloved hands and placed it in a Styrofoam container. But as we returned to the trailer, I was stunned to see her children playing with another cub.

"Where did *that* one come from?" I asked.

The woman's face fell into a gaping scowl. "I thought I told you kids to stay put!" she shouted, which caused her dogs to erupt into a chaotic chorus of earsplitting howls.

"SHAD UP! SHHHAAAAD UP!" she hollered. Stooping, she picked up a handful of stones and hurled them one by one at the dogs until they retreated into their sweltering huts.

She marched over to her children, her broad shadow enveloping them. "You'll both be punished for this!"

"Ma'am," I said. "Where did you get the raccoons?"

She turned and raised a hand to block the sun. "A friend found them when he was stacking field stone," she said squinting at me. "They were abandoned, so he kept one and gave us the other two." She nodded at the box in my hand. "That one died in about three days. The other one is doing fine. My kids love her to death. She's a girl, you know."

"What's your friend's name?"

She frowned. "What do you want to know that for?"

I glanced at the children, my expression grim.

"You kids get in the house, right now!" she scolded.

The girl with the bandaged arm quickly picked up the cub as both girls disappeared into their dim trailer.

"We have a rabies problem in Wyoming County," I said. "If the dead cub was infected, the other one might be too. Besides, it's illegal to take animals from the wild. I can't let you keep it."

"But how are we supposed to know about a law like that? Besides, Ned said that the cubs didn't have a mama."

"Ned?"

"Ned Viper. He lives over the county line about a mile from here. Are you gonna take our baby away?"

"I don't have a choice, ma'am. It has to be tested for rabies. If the animal is infected your daughter will need a series of shots right away."

Her brow arched. "Shots? I'll bet they're expensive!"

"Several hundred at least."

"Several hundred!" She stared at me as if all of this were my fault. "How am I supposed to pay for that?"

"The raccoon probably isn't infected," I said in an attempt to console her. "The test is more a precaution then anything."

"What kind of test? What are they gonna do?"

I looked at her. My expression conveying bad news.

"You're gonna kill it . . . ?"

"No choice. The lab has to examine brain tissue to determine if the virus is present. Rabies is a fatal disease. Sorry, but your family's health takes precedence."

She turned abruptly and marched into her trailer. I could hear everything through the thin walls: "Girls, come here and bring Bandit," she called gruffly "We gotta give her to the game warden."

"But why mommy? Why?" they pleaded.

"Because she might be sick, and he wants her."

"What's going to happen to Bandit, mommy?" they cried. "Will she go to a doctor and get all better again?"

"She ain't going to a doctor and she ain't getting better!" The game warden is gonna kill her. That's what game wardens do!" She stormed out of her trailer with the cub clenched firmly by the nape of its neck and thrust her arm at me. "Go on, take it!"

The cub started to bawl in pitiful, high-pitched squeals, sending her dogs into a yowling frenzy once again as I took the bewildered animal from her and stared into the tearful eyes of her daughters. I wanted to comfort them somehow, tell them everything would be all right, but it would have been a lie. And so, with a heavy heart, I turned and walked to my patrol car amidst the gasping sobs of children and the mindless barking of dogs.

After delivering the cubs to the state lab, I radioed Chuck "Arco" Arcovitch. Ned Viper lived in Arco's district, so I briefed him on what had happened and arranged to meet him on my way to collect the third cub.

It was a twenty-mile drive to Viper's place, and as I followed Arco's patrol car into his driveway, I spotted an old Chevy backed in close to Viper's house, as if ready to make a quick getaway. There was a man sitting behind the steering wheel. Another man stood next to the car, facing him in deep conversation. He looked up and spotted us, then turned abruptly and began walking away. Suspecting the raccoon might be inside the car, Chuck stopped in front of the Chevy to block it while I quickly parked behind him and jumped out.

Arco reached the vehicle seconds ahead of me and spotted a rifle on the front seat. He ordered the driver to keep his hands on the steering wheel, but instead the man reached down and hooked the bolt of his rifle with a thumb, snapping it open

"It's empty, you idiot!" he barked. "I'm on private property and you got no right to harass me here. Now you better get the hell out of my way because I'm leaving!"

Again Arco ordered the man to put his hands on the steering wheel, and when he saw me reaching for the passenger door from the corner of his eye, he quickly complied. I jerked the door open and took the rifle. Arco warned him to keep his hands where we could see them, explaining that we were investigating a game law violation.

"I ain't got nothing in my car. You can see that!" the man cried. "What are you hassling me for?"

"If you're not doing anything wrong, I guess you wouldn't mind if we take a look in your trunk," said Arco.

The man glared at him, his eyes fixed and brooding. Then, without another word, he slid from his vehicle and walked around to the trunk. He opened it, revealing nothing but a spare tire and a few shop tools. "See! Just like I told you!"

Arco demanded some identification. And with remarkable obedience, the man reached into his back pocket and pulled out a bedraggled wallet. Pinching the corner of his driver's license with blackened fingers he handed it to him.

After copying the name and address in a notebook, Arco returned his license. "You were just leaving, right?"

"That's what I've been trying to tell you!" He grinned at us with teeth rotting from neglect. "And I want my rifle back, too"

I handed him his empty rifle. Then, without another word, he got back into his car and sped down the narrow driveway onto the hardtop. We watched him go, his car fading into the steamy heat-shimmer like an apparition.

Arco and I quickly turned our attention to the other man. He and a female companion were watching us. They lounged upon plastic reclining chairs on their front lawn, drinking cans of beer in the blazing sun. Surrounded by acres of weeds that hadn't seen a mower in weeks, they looked utterly absurd, as if basking in a vast and tortured wasteland.

We walked over. A small wooden table stood between them encircled by a dozen empty beer cans casually strewn about. On the table was a half-full pack of Camels and a tin ashtray crammed with cigarette butts.

"What do you two want?" grunted Viper. Straw-like hair spilled past his collar to meld with his dense beard and mustache. He wore glasses with thin round rims—just like Ben Franklin—and a cotton shirt with faded jeans (Arco later told me that to him, Viper looked just like the infamous Claude Lafayette Dallas who was convicted of shooting two game wardens to death in Nevada several years earlier).

Arco said, "We understand you gave a raccoon cub to a woman in Wyoming County and that you have another one somewhere on your property, is that true?"

Viper sprang to his feet, his face contorted with rage. "You got no right on my property! This ain't nothing but harassment. I don't have to answer any of your questions. Now, get off my land and leave me alone!"

Once again, we found ourselves in a hostile environment. To make matters worse, two young boys suddenly appeared from out of the house—Viper's sons, perhaps—and walked over to us. Thinking things could get out of hand and not wanting to subject them to Viper's reckless behavior, I said, "How about we get out of the sun and take a walk over to my car."

Viper's head whipped toward me. "I don't have to go anywhere with you." His eyes darted nervously to Arco, then back to me, and I sensed something was about to happen.

Suddenly he did an about face and set his beer can on the table. My heart leaped when I saw the forty-five caliber pistol jutting from the beltline in the small of his back.

"Hold it right there!" I cried, going for my revolver.

Viper's back was still toward me as he reached around and grabbed the butt of his pistol. "Talking about this?" he said over his shoulder.

My thumb was pushing frantically against the leather snap that secured my gun inside my holster, but it wouldn't open. From where Arco was standing, he couldn't see Viper's pistol, and I watched in horror as he pulled the weapon from his belt. It all happened so fast—in a heartbeat he had a gun in his hand and could have killed us both.

Instead, keeping his back to me, Viper deliberately laid his pistol flat on the table and stepped away from it. Arco sprang forward and snatched it. He ejected the magazine into his hand, then jerked back the slide. A live round whirled in the air, its brass casing glistening in the sun. Arco reached out and caught it. He dropped it into his pocket, then tucked the empty weapon into his belt. We each grabbed an arm and escorted Viper to my vehicle, away from his wife and children.

"Hey!" he squawked. "Lighten up. What's wrong with you guys?"

"You're lucky you weren't shot!" I snapped back at him.

And indeed he likely would have been, except a poorly designed thumb-break on my holster had prevented me from drawing my gun (the agency went with an improved holster design that included a more rigid thumb break after my incident with Viper).

Arco ordered Viper to turn around. He frisked him for additional weapons while I covered him. Satisfied he was clean, Arco's eyes bored into Viper, his voice low and even. "We're here to talk to you about a raccoon, and you start cursing us and pull a gun . . . ! For what?"

Viper raised his palms defensively, "Okay, okay already. But I ain't got no coon, man. You can look all you want; I got nothing to hide. I'll take you on the Grand Tour myself."

Ned Viper had his faults, but stupidity wasn't one of them. He wouldn't have offered to show us around if a raccoon was anywhere in sight.

We followed him more out of morbid curiosity than anything as he led us through several outbuildings, each with their own assortment of farm tools, rusty machinery, and odd junk. As suspected, we saw no sign of a raccoon or animal cages anywhere. "C'mon," Viper offered cheerily. "I'll show you inside my house, too." And with a dim sense of reluctance, Arco and I trailed him into his rundown trailer.

Here the shades were drawn, giving the place all the charm of an ancient burial chamber, the gloomy atmosphere mirroring Ned Viper to a tee. Several small tables were scattered about, each piled with its own assortment of dirty rags, old newspapers, and other useless articles. Against a far wall, a raggedy wooden desk was crammed with reloading equipment and empty shell casings, indicating Viper's passion for shooting.

After sidestepping an assortment of dated newspapers and magazines scattered across the floor, we followed him into another room and our eyes focused on an extensive collection of brutish, gothic-style knives and swords that hung on every wall.

"See? No raccoon!" said Viper. "But I do have other pets. Come and look."

Centered on an old card table we saw a small glass aquarium. Inside, an enormous tarantula crouched. Viper reached in and pulled the hairy creature from its prison. "This one is my favorite."

Its long, segmented legs groped hideously, turning my spine to jelly. He extended his arm and offered the trashing spider to me. "Wanna hold 'em?"

I felt my flesh begin to crawl. "I'd rather have an eye gouged out," I assured him.

Viper cocked his head and eyed me hurtfully. Then he shrugged and plopped the tarantula back into its aquarium. "Suit yourself."

Ned Viper continued leading us through his dingy trailer until we eventually walked out the back door.

Arco turned to face him. "I don't know what you did with the raccoon but Officer Wasserman and I are leaving."

Viper grinned broadly as Arco handed him his gun. But his expression quickly turned sour when he realized it had been disassembled. "What the . . . !"

"Don't worry," said Arco, "You'll find your slide, empty magazine, and nine rounds on the table next to your hairy friend inside."

Although we didn't find a raccoon cub at Ned Viper's place, Arco later charged him with the unlawful possession of wildlife and subpoenaed the woman whose child had been bitten to testify against him as a Commonwealth witness. But rather than go through a lengthy trial, Viper pled guilty and paid his fine in full.

Later that summer, we heard Viper had an unwelcomed encounter with several members of a rival outlaw motorcycle gang and that he went into hiding in rural New York. Perhaps it's no coincidence that we never ran into him again after that day.

Outlaws at Wildcat Ridge

His HEADLIGHTS FLICKERED between the trees, casting ghostly shadows into the woods as he crept down the narrow two-track. It was a cold and moonless November night, and his heart beat in heavy anticipation. The trail camera he'd set up behind his house had been triggered each morning for days. The buck in the photographs enormous.

There were other deer too. Many of them. But it was the heavy eight-pointer with the unusually wide rack that had captivated Eli Bragg.

He brought his pickup to a stop fifty yards from a large pile of fresh corn and shut off the lights. He killed the ignition, leaned back in his seat, and listened to the steady tick of his cooling engine. Daylight was close at hand. Soon the buck would appear, drawn to his bait as surely as a fly is drawn to sugar.

As the darkness began to melt into a gray dawn, the deer suddenly materialized. Captivated by its presence, Bragg's thick fingers tightened around the steering wheel. His time had come. With the season only two days away, the woods would soon be crawling with eager hunters. Some of them his best friends. And Eli Bragg was about to make certain none of them got a chance to take his trophy away.

Having grown accustomed to the bait, the buck paid no attention to him. And when the poacher switched on his headlights, the whitetail raised its head in mild curiosity to gaze into the blinding abyss, its antlers immense in the blazing glare of light.

Eli Bragg raised his twenty-two magnum off the seat, poked the muzzle out his open window, and settled the wooden stock into his right shoulder. He sucked in a long breath as the crosshairs found their mark, then he exhaled slowly and squeezed the trigger.

The rifle cracked like lightning, its deadly missile boring through the deer's head, belching splinters of skull and bits of brain into the air. The great buck dropped to the ground like a puppet whose strings had been cut from above, its hind legs raking the earth as Eli Bragg rested his gun on the seat. He waited for the deer to stop moving, then he started his engine and drove over to collect his prize.

The following day, my neighboring officer, Jim Jolly, happened to be flying over his district in search of illegal bait. As the chopper approached the Wyoming County line, it skirted Wildcat Ridge and was about to head back when something caught Jolly's eye. He signaled the pilot to circle. From the air, piles of bright yellow corn could be seen in the naked woods behind Eli Bragg's house. It was the only bait he'd been able to locate all morning. Because it was in my district, Jolly contacted me by landline as soon as he returned to his office, and we arranged to meet the following day.

With our vehicles hidden behind an abandoned barn a half-mile from Bragg's house, Jolly and I hiked through the woods until we reached the back of his property and came to a well-established Jeep trail. We followed it, stunned by what we found: Dotting the trail at fifty-yard intervals were six wooden structures the size of large coat closets. They were enclosed deer blinds with golf ball sized peepholes bored through their walls for shooting at game. Across from each blind, a bushel-sized wire basket filled with corncobs had been nailed to a tree.

We pushed deeper into the property, taking photographs of the bait and the blinds as we went. Soon we came upon two weather-beaten travel trailers sitting on cinder blocks at the edge of a meadow. A truckload of corncobs had been dumped nearby. I peeked inside each trailer. Wooden gun benches had been built under their windows, providing a steady surface for shooters to brace their aim.

Three more baited blinds were positioned within the nearby woods. They were large wooden structures big enough for two occupants. Inside we found cushioned chairs and propane heaters to make things cozy, and they had sliding glass windows for shooting at game lured to the corn and salt blocks that stood a short distance away.

Jolly and I continued along the two-track until we discovered the main camp: a rustic two-story cabin with all the comforts of home, it had four separate rooms with comfy bunk beds and a cozy, well-equipped kitchen. A glass structure protruded through the shingled roof like a chimney. It was an overlook big enough for a man to stand in and had windows that could be raised for easy gunning. Below the structure, two shooting lanes had been cut through the woods, with every tree removed in six-foot-wide swaths, providing corridors for shooting at anything that moved.

Positioned fifty yards from the cabin was an automatic grain feeder bursting with corn. It had been built from a five-foot wooden reel. The kind used by power companies for rolling out electric wire. We found fresh blood and turkey feathers under the feeder, indicating recent illegal kills. Nearby, several bucket-sized salt blocks sat on tree stumps, each surrounded by a blanket of shelled corn twenty feet in diameter.

From here, a short walk along the trail brought us to two wooden outhouses. We were amazed to see peepholes had been drilled through the doors so game could be shot even under the most trying of circumstances.

Jolly and I continued walking along the trail until we rounded a broad bend and stumbled upon another cabin with a mountain of corn stacked just outside. There were no vehicles around, so we moved in to investigate. The place wasn't as big or as well equipped as the first cabin; it served more as a crude bunkhouse than anything. It was a two-tiered wooden structure, the first floor containing four beds, a potbellied coal stove, and some metal folding chairs. The upper section was empty except for a wooden rifle-bench located under a sliding window for shooting at game.

Through the distant morning haze, we could see Bragg's house: a modest ranch home situated at the edge of a paved township road. The two-track led from the woods directly to his back yard where it merged with his driveway. It was the only way into the baited blinds by motor vehicle. Because anyone coming from this direction had to pass within twenty feet of Bragg's front door, he must have felt confident that he'd never be caught. And considering what Jolly and I had just discovered, he'd been poaching game with impunity for many years.

Satisfied we had seen enough to launch a successful raid, we went back the same way we came in and quickly departed.

Later that afternoon, I was sitting at my desk formulating a strategy for the following day when the phone rang.

It was our agency dispatcher, his tone uncharacteristically glum. "Got a call from a TV news reporter who wants to follow you around tomorrow with a cameraman," he said. "He's looking for a story on the first day of buck season."

The dispatcher knew that a TV journalist tagging along would only add to the craziness that comes with the opening day. An unwelcomed burden to be sure. Typically, I'd be run ragged trying to keep up with complaints about trespassing, mistake kills, road hunting, injured deer, and countless other calls. After all, the county was about to be set upon by thousands of avid hunters—the good, the bad, and the ugly, so to speak. And so he never expected my response.

"Good!" I said. "Tell him to meet me at five tomorrow morning in the Walmart parking lot."

"You sound grateful! Must have something going on."

"I sure do. And it should make for some good footage."

"I'll pass it along, Bill. Good luck tomorrow."

Buck season rolled in with a steady light rain as Deputy Jeff Pierce and I cruised north on Route Twenty-nine. The headlights in my rearview mirror told me TV news reporter Drew Mitchell and his cameraman were close behind.

After a thirty-minute drive, we reached our rendezvous point and I pulled in and parked. It was still pitch black outside. Jim Jolly was standing by his patrol car, a thermos of coffee on the hood. A group of deputies stood along with him. I took a quick count: twelve men would be moving in on Eli Bragg's bait stations. I hadn't expected Jolly to bring so many reinforcements, but I was glad he did.

Deputy Gene Gaydos, my sentry, had been hidden for hours on a bleak hilltop where he could listen for shots and watch vehicles entering or exiting Bragg's property with his binoculars. I shivered when I considered the icy drizzle he'd endured. Grabbing my mike, I radioed him for status.

His familiar voice crackled back. "No shots fired and no headlights indicating travel into or out of the camp, Bill."

The news surprised me. I had Gaydos watching the place because I expected the shooting would start before sunrise. I also anticipated a stream of vehicles would have moved in by now. It didn't seem right.

I looked at Pierce. "If we go in there like gangbusters and the place is empty, it's really gonna look bad."

"Especially when they run it on the six o'clock news," he grunted. He rolled down his window and stuck out a hand. "Oh well, at least it stopped raining."

As dawn began to break, I called the troops together under a dismal gray sky and briefed them on what to expect when they entered Bragg's property. I had them team up in pairs, four men to a vehicle, with each vehicle assigned specific blinds to inspect.

My marked patrol car was in the lead as we steered into Bragg's driveway. News Reporter Drew Mitchell and his video technician were with me, the cameraman cradling his equipment tightly in his arms as my patrol car brushed past Eli Bragg's house, hit the two-track, and traveled across a rough and broken meadow into the woods. We reached the first structure in seconds. It was the two-tier blind with the mountain of corn out front—the last baited blind that Jolly and I had found the day before. A light shined in a window, confirming that someone was inside.

I veered left toward the structure. The other vehicles pushing past me, deeper into the woods.

I parked and jumped out. In five broad steps I reached the door and rapped on it with a hard fist. "State Game Commission!" I cried. "Come out!"

There was the scrape of a chair, the shuffle of heavy feet coming my way. When the door opened, a man in his early fifties stood before me, his burly outline consuming every inch of the frame. He eyed the cameraman uneasily as he filmed us, his bulky video machine perched on one shoulder.

"State game warden," I said. "We're here to investigate unlawful hunting activity."

He saw my team swarming though the woods behind me. Men in uniform moved quickly toward the remaining blinds deeper into the property. His expression turned grim. "I'm

Eli Bragg," he said. He nodded toward the door. "Why don't we step inside. I'd like to talk privately."

I followed him into the wooden building, my eyes searching for anyone else who might be inside. An old potbelly woodstove sat by the far wall, its iron door ajar. I could see the warm glow of burning embers inside. On the floor next to the stove, I spotted a bloody ribcage protruding from a metal feed pan. Bragg glanced at the remains. "That's just a roadkill. Picked it up two days ago."

I'd heard the excuse a hundred times before from a hundred different men. I let it pass. There was a window behind Bragg. I invited him to look outside. He watched uneasily as my deputies escorted several camo-clad hunters toward the main camp. Bragg turned to me and rubbed a heavily whiskered cheek. "I want to know if we can work something out," he said flatly.

"We're not going to work anything out unless you start telling the truth," I said. "You can begin with that ribcage."

Bragg stared at me for a moment, then he shuffled back to a dim corner of the room, bent down, and pulled a cardboard box from under a bed. It contained the head of an exceptional eight-point buck. "You're right," he said. "It ain't no roadkill. Would've made a dandy trophy, too. I shot it Saturday night."

Bragg told me about how he'd been watching the deer come to his bait for weeks. "Couldn't help myself," he shrugged. "Prettiest set of horns I ever saw."

"Appreciate your honesty," I said. "Do you have any concealed weapons on you?"

"Nope. Couple of rifles upstairs, though. Look around if you want."

I searched the building, found two empty rifles, and took them out to my vehicle along with the illegal deer head. Bragg stood outside and watched me. He turned his face away when the cameraman tried to catch him on film. "Does the whole world have to know about this?" he griped.

"That's not my call," I said. "Let's take a walk over to your cabin. See who your friends are."

Four men gawked in comic disbelief as we approached along with Drew Mitchell and his cameraman. It had all happened so quickly: the game wardens had swooped in and plucked them from their cozy blinds before they could even think. And now a TV camera was rolling while Officer Jolly briefed me on what he and the deputies had found.

Eli Bragg's son, Eliza, who looked to be in his mid-thirties, had been discovered hiding in a baited blind, ten yards from a bushel of corncobs. Two others, Truman Cheat and his son, Ernest, were picked up in separate blinds a short distance away. The fourth suspect, Louis Loud, was caught inside one of the travel trailers as he peeked out at a quarter ton of corn. All had loaded rifles.

As I informed the men that the entire property was off-limits to hunting until every grain of bait was removed and thirty days had passed, Eliza Bragg protested vehemently. "It's our land!" he whined. "We should be able to hunt the way we want. You got no right to be trespassing here."

"Wrong," I said. "You might own the land, but you don't own the wildlife. Citations will be coming in the mail. But you can always take a hearing. See what the judge thinks."

I turned to Truman and Ernest Cheat. They were about the same age as Eli Bragg and his son. Standing at rigid attention, they stared at the ground hoping they wouldn't see their faces on tonight's evening news. "Anything to say?"

Both men shook their heads without looking up. Meanwhile, soft-spoken Louis Loud smiled amiably for the news camera and asked me how much his fine would be so he could pay it and go home.

"You're not going anywhere until we're finished," I said. I turned to Eli Bragg. "Still willing to talk?"

Bragg hesitated a moment. Then he pursed his lips, nodded sideways, and motioned me into his cabin.

As we took seats in the cabin's warm kitchen, Bragg leaned back in his chair and popped open the lid of an adjacent woodstove. He took an oak log from a pile on the floor and dropped it inside. The fire crackled and sparked wildly. "What do you want to know?" he asked, turning toward me.

"Everything," I said.

The poacher crossed both arms leisurely over his wide belly and laced his fingers together. A big man, he wore a red and black checkered hunting shirt with suspenders that were stretched to the breaking point. He regarded me for a long moment, musing, it seemed, over his options. Then his pale blue eyes brightened sharply. "You got me," he chuckled softly. "You got all of us!"

I nodded in agreement.

"Okay," he said. "Ask away."

Wire basket with corncobs used to bait deer.

I pulled a tape-recorder from my briefcase and placed it on the kitchen table. "Mind if I record what you say?"

Bragg thought for a moment and then shrugged indifferently. "Go ahead," he said. "I'm just gonna tell you the truth, anyway." He ran a thick hand through his tangled hair and turned to gaze out the window. A wire basket filled with corn had been nailed to a tree just outside. To Eli Bragg, poaching was as natural as slipping into his favorite hunting boots, and I suppose I should have felt a strong resentment toward him. But he possessed an unexpected amiable quality that made him more tolerable than most outlaws I've met.

So there would be no challenge from a defense attorney if his confession was introduced in court, I pushed the record button and asked if he was aware that he was being taped. He answered yes. Next, I informed him of his right to remain silent under the law. He nodded he understood, so I started my interrogation by asking about the eight-point buck he'd killed. Bragg held nothing back. He admitted shooting it through the headlights of his pickup while it fed on the bait he'd put out, adding that the venison had been ground up and put in his freezer. I was welcome to it, he said. No search warrant would be necessary.

"Appreciate your cooperation," I replied. "Now, let's switch gears a little. How many turkeys did you kill over bait?"

The corners of Bragg's mouth drew down in a gesture of mock surprise. "Turkeys . . . ?"

"We found blood and feathers under your grain feeder."

Bragg stared out the kitchen window. He shook his head wearily. "Man, you guys are thorough, I'll say that. I killed three this year. One in the spring, two this fall."

He caught me off guard. I expected him to only admit to one turkey. It seemed like he wanted to talk, so I pressed my luck: "This isn't the first time you've done this, is it, Eli?"

"Nope. Been shooting deer here for eight years."

Stunned by the admission, I kept a straight face. I wanted Bragg to think I knew more about his camp then I actually did—that my questions, for the most part, were a mere formality, thereby encouraging him to speak more freely.

"Bet you've killed a lot of game in all that time."

"Yep."

"How many deer and turkeys would that be?"

Bragg's eyes rolled upwards while mentally counting. It took him a few seconds to come up with a number: "One deer each year," he said, "and probably two turkeys along with that."

I leaned back on my chair and tried to look unmoved by his confession. "That would be eight deer and seventeen turkeys including the three birds you killed this year. Sound about right?"

"Yeah, I guess so."

I jotted the information down on a notepad. "How much corn have you brought into your camp this year?"

He leaned toward me as if in grand confidence, both elbows on the table. "I just brought a truckload in the other day; paid a hundred dollars for it. That was about a ton."

"A ton . . . ?"

Bragg shrugged at my astonishment. "There's nothing else for them to feed on around here," he reasoned. "This past year I put corn out all winter long—seven tons. Been doing it every year for the past eight. I only have twenty acres. The neighbors won't let us hunt on their land—they were shooting us out! So I decided to do something about it. Cost me a fortune, but we brought in the game."

It began to make more sense. Bragg's property bordered a huge corporate landholding. The landowners refused to allow him access, so he came up with a plan to lure the game off their property onto his own small tract of land.

"Speaking of costs, you're looking at a substantial fine," I said.

"Figured as much. What are we talking about?"

"For you, over a thousand. Your buddies are looking at two hundred apiece unless we uncover more violations. And there will likely be hunting licenses revoked as well." I paused for a moment to let it all sink in. "You have the right to a trial on all this, you know. Everybody does."

"Nope! I'll just pay my fine," he said coolly. "I'll tell the rest of the men to pay too. I think you're being fair with us."

After obtaining a written confession from Bragg, I stepped back outside to address his companions. I explained the penalty each man was facing along with his option to simply pay the fine or take a trial before a district judge. My team then gathered all firearms and other paraphernalia in the event of a court case. But before we departed, Jim Jolly handed me a videotape he'd found in Truman Cheat's blind. I tucked it in my coat pocket and planned to view it later.

Eli Bragg was looking at a thirteen-hundred dollar fine for hunting over bait and the unlawful killing of one deer and one turkey. Although he'd confessed to killing many other deer and turkeys, Pennsylvania law prohibits police from filing charges on most crimes and offenses over two years old. Additionally, I lacked any real evidence other than Bragg's confession, which is not enough, in itself, to convict someone in a court of law. Still, the outlaw gang was facing thousands in fines, and for some, a lifetime of illegal hunting had finally caught up with them.

The video that Officer Jolly had seized almost put me to sleep as I sat on my couch staring at the TV screen. An entire week had passed since the raid. Deer season had kept me on the go almost constantly, and it was the first chance I had to look at it.

It had been running for thirty minutes. Early scenes depicting a few antlerless deer milling around a wooden corn feeder. Later footage showed a bunch of turkeys under the same feeder. The film had been taken over a period of days, its tiresome footage always the same: either a small band of deer or a flock of turkeys eating corn like common farm stock. Pretty boring stuff, to say the least.

Until a gunshot suddenly rang out.

I was jolted to the edge of my seat as a large gobbler went cartwheeling from the flock, wings pumping wildly upon the forest floor. It soon stopped moving altogether, its body deflating into a lifeless heap as the remaining flock scattered helter-skelter into the woods.

Then voices began to emerge from the video. Low, whispering sounds. I recognized them instantly:

"I don't care what anybody says," breathed Eli Bragg. "You can't beat them danged twenty-two magnums!"

"Yeah, they're nice all right," agreed Truman Cheat, his voice equally low. "—Hey, those birds didn't get too far.

How 'bout we leave that one lay and wait for the others to come back . . ."

The film blipped for a moment, ending this segment before going on to show Eli Bragg and his son Eliza along with Truman Cheat. They were a happy bunch, full of smiles and good-natured boasting in front of the camera as Eliza Bragg held a dead gobbler by its feet. I rewound the tape and wondered how many more creatures they had killed like this over the years. I supposed it might be a hundred or more.

When Eli Bragg strolled into the State Police barracks and stated that he was there to see me, a state trooper escorted him down a narrow hallway into a vacant room where I sat at a long conference table, a television at one end.

"Must be pretty important to bring me here on a workday," he huffed.

I picked up a remote control, pointed it at the TV, and pushed the play button.

Bragg folded his arms across his chest and turned his head to watch. His jaw tightened, eyes glued to the screen, as he witnessed a turkey go cartwheeling across the ground. I shut off the set and looked up at him. "Look familiar?"

"Okay," he said flatly. "How much is *this* gonna cost?"

"You're looking at another six hundred."

"Fair enough," he replied, shaking his head wearily. "You got me right there on television for crying out loud!"

Eli's son was next. "You stole that tape!" he cried when it was over. "You got no right to have it!"

I shook my head. "You have a strange perspective about life, Eliza. You're the one poaching game and robbing honest hunters—but I'm the thief, right?"

"I'll see you in court, and when this is over I'm gonna sue you for violating my hunting rights!" Then he pivoted and went for the door. A trooper stood waiting to escort him outside. I was glad to see him depart.

Truman Cheat was last to watch. He sat numbly, witnessing his big film debut in wide-eyed disbelief.

"I can't believe we taped this stuff," he muttered when it ended. "You got us cold. What kind of fine am I looking at?"

I hit the remote, shutting down the TV. "Before I saw this video, you were facing one charge of hunting over bait. Of course, things have changed considerably. We have you on film assisting to kill a turkey over bait. Looks like your fine just jumped from two hundred to over a thousand dollars."

Cheat winced painfully and shook his head. "Any chance you could give me a break? That's a lot of money."

The man was a career poacher. How many creatures had he killed illegally in his life? The number had to be staggering. Yet he wanted leniency from me.

"I don't think so. But you have the right to a trial—"

"Oh forget that!" snapped Cheat. "I don't want to go to court! You guys got us. I'll just pay the fine—that's all I can do. That's all any of us can do."

Louis Loud and Earnest Cheat paid their fines and had their hunting and trapping privileges revoked for one year. Eliza Bragg decided not to hire an attorney after all, and paid his six-hundred dollar fine. He received two years revocation. Eli Bragg made payments on his seventeen-hundred dollar fine for many, many months. His hunting and trapping privileges were revoked for seven years, and I never ran into him again.

Truman Cheat pled guilty, paid his fine, and received five years revocation of his hunting and trapping privileges. However, I arrested him again for killing a buck in closed season shortly after he got his license back. It happened in an open field in broad daylight. A witness had watched him from afar and then contacted me right away.

It was a first step. Evidently the TV news broadcast and subsequent newspaper stories about the outlaws at Wildcat Ridge had helped folks appreciate what was going on there. The routine slaughter of innocent wildlife didn't set well with them. As a result, the place is no longer a haven for poachers, and the deer and turkeys are thriving once again.

The Killers

THE FIRST THING HE NOTICED when he woke up was that he had a splitting headache. Like his skull had been stuck inside a giant vice while some sicko screwed the jaws tighter and tighter. He gazed at the ceiling. What was he doing lying on the couch? Must have passed out!

He could hear voices in the distance. Garbled at first, they gradually drifted closer over the surging pain Suddenly everything began coming back to him. He could remember drinking shots and beers with Drago and Lennie. An argument broke out. Then what?—That's right! They were fighting over money. Drug money. Drago pulled out a hunting knife as Lennie charged at him in a fit of rage. But Lennie never saw Slater and Lavar. They were on him in seconds, smashing his head into the table while Drago finished him with his blade.

It all started coming back to him. He'd tried to stop them. Tried to help Lennie. But Lavar saw him coming and shoved a bent knee into his guts. He doubled over and started sucking wind. After that, everything went black . . .

He cut his eyes to the left. They were sitting at a card table, their backs hunched toward him, deep in conversation. A dark crimson stain anointed the carpet next to them.

Blood!

Lennie's blood!

And as he listened to the three men, feigning unconsciousness, a thick and deepening terror swarmed into his chest. Their conversation was about *him!* The men he planned to go deer hunting with had murdered Lennie, and now they were plotting to kill their only witness.

Lavar laced his fingers over the back of his head and leaned back through the cigarette and cigar smoke that hung in the air like a fog. "The way I see it, we got no choice. We gotta kill him. He saw us do Lennie."

Drago slapped his hand firmly on the table. "Agreed! Besides, we can get rid of two bodies easy as one. But we finish him outside. I don't want no more mess in here."

"We're wasting time," Slater grumbled. "It'll be easier if we take care of him before he wakes up."

The conversation seemed impossible! He had to escape! His eyes strained through the dim wash of light. Their rifles were still in gun racks on the far wall. Hopefully empty. No one planned to hunt until tomorrow.

Although woozy from his head injury, odds were still good he'd be gone before they could stop him. Their backs were turned, and they'd been drinking heavily. He'd have to go without his coat; but taking a chance on dying from the elements was better than facing certain death in the cabin.

He sprang from the couch and leaped toward the back door, yanking it open. The frigid air was like a slap in the face, the darkness and snow turning everything black and white. An icy spot caught him as he fled. His legs shot out from under him. He went down fast and hit his head hard, losing valuable seconds.

He sprang to his feet and looked back.

Someone was coming!

It was Slater. And he had a rifle in his hands.

He sprinted wildly down the narrow Jeep trail, knowing all the while that Slater was a crack shot. No way he could outrun a bullet. The nerves in his spine bunched into an excruciating knot as he imagined a lead slug slamming into his back. He ran for his life, the full moon illuminating the snowscape, its shadows playing eerily among the naked oak and beech trees. He had only gone a hundred yards when the combination of his utter panic and poor physical condition began to take their toll. His legs were cement. His lungs heaved. His entire body drenched in sweat.

He chanced a look back.

No one there.

He doubled over and retched. Then, in the distance, there came a rough mechanical whine advancing quickly.

An ATV!

Slater had just upped the odds five-hundred percent!

He scanned the terrain, searching frantically for cover.

A snowdrift! His only chance. He dove behind it . . .

Hours passed before he moved a muscle. He must have blacked out again. Ironically, he thought, Slater, Drago, and Lavar might just get their wish. It would be perfect, too. They'd find him dead and frozen solid in the morning.

The bitter cold was unbearable. He had to get down the mountain. His clothes were wet and his body shook convulsively. If he didn't find help, hypothermia, and then death, would be inevitable. He stood slowly and looked back toward the cabin. Lights were out. The men finally asleep.

Willing deadened legs to stir, he began to stagger forward in a pathetic, lurching gate . . .

I was taken aback when I picked up the phone. Late hour calls the night before buck season are usually about poaching, not murder.

"Bill, this is Chet Goldyn at the barracks," said a familiar voice. "We have someone here claiming there's been a homicide at a cabin in a remote section of the county. We think the suspects are still out there and could use an extra man with a four-wheel-drive vehicle."

The state troopers and I had joined forces many times over the years, but this would be my first assist on a murder investigation. "How soon do you need me?"

"Right now."

"I'll get a uniform on and be right over."

When I arrived at the barracks, Trooper Goldyn was sitting at a desk questioning a weary and disheveled looking man seated in front of him. He wrote down information on a legal pad as the man answered his questions.

Corporal George Meyers saw me walk in and stepped out of his office into the narrow corridor. "Thanks for coming,

Bill," he said. His expression was grave. "The man we're interviewing just walked out of the hospital. He'd been in the emergency room with hypothermia. Two hunters found him wandering around yesterday morning without a coat, apparently delirious. Hospital said his body temperature was dangerously low. Said he's lucky someone found him when they did. The man claims his hunting buddies murdered someone named Lennie June. Then they went after him, but he managed to escape."

Corporal Meyers filled me in on the rest of the story, then leaned back against the wall and folded his arms across his chest. "I don't know," he muttered reflectively. "He seems believable, but he also admits he'd been drinking heavily when all this took place." He turned and stared into the interrogation room where Trooper Goldyn continued to question the witness. "Something must have happened up there," he said, his tone indicating he wasn't quite sure what, however. He started toward his office, then turned abruptly and faced me. "By the way, we checked criminal records on the men at the cabin. They're tied in with an outlaw motorcycle gang in Philadelphia . . ."

Two marked patrol cars made their way slowly up the winding mountain road. Corporal Meyers was in the lead, driving a PSP Jeep Cherokee. Three troopers accompanied him. I followed in my state-issued Bronco. We traveled totally in the dark, without headlights. And because a thick cloud-covering obscured any hint of moonlight, we almost missed the two-track that cut to our right and led to the suspects' cabin. The narrow road was a mixture of greasy mud and wet snow that sucked our tires into an endless sinking mire. We ascended another hundred yards or so, when the trail suddenly turned to a sheet of solid ice. Progress, even by four-wheel-drive, became impossible. We stopped, grabbed our equipment, and bailed out.

We would continue from here on foot. Make our way to the cabin and determine if it was still occupied. The plan was to move in quickly and take control of the suspects. For our own safety, we had to assume they were armed and dangerous. But as long as they didn't see us coming, we'd have the element of surprise on our side.

Troopers Jeff Ceccarelli and Chad Cunningham formed the reconnaissance team. Armed with assault rifles and night scopes, the two young officers roamed forward, their black garb soon melting into the darkness. They were to make an exploratory survey of the territory, scouting ahead to ensure our raid would be unexpected.

After giving them a ten-minute lead, we moved forward. Walking was extremely difficult—each step a deliberate effort to secure footing. The temperature was dropping fast. By the time we reached the top, it would likely be in the low teens. My topographical map indicated we were at one thousand feet elevation—their cabin, twenty-one hundred. With the frozen conditions, our trek would only become more challenging as we pushed ahead.

Suddenly our portable radio came alive. It was recon. Although the message was broken and scratchy, we could pick up Ceccarelli's distant voice.

He was warning us to stay back!

We froze in our tracks, eyes searching into the black surround.

Trooper Goldyn barked at his handheld: "Recon, are you all right?"

Seconds passed like hours as we waited for a response.

"Affirmative," came the reply at last "Stay put. We're coming in."

Soon two shadowy figures appeared like apparitions before us. It was Ceccarelli and Cunningham. They told us they'd discovered three pickup trucks parked along the trail ahead. The vehicles had too much distance between them to be inspected safely by just two men. They needed backup.

We followed the troopers into the gloom until the trucks' hulking frames materialized on the trail ahead. Breaking into three teams, we moved forward cautiously, checking each vehicle for occupants. All were empty. Corporal Meyers called in the license numbers. Headquarters came back with the information in minutes: the plates belonged to Drago, Slater, and Lavar. The three men had evidently walked to the cabin from here.

The report confirmed one thing for certain: our suspects would still be there when we arrived.

Once again, recon pushed ahead while we followed at a safe distance. Travel became more treacherous with every bend in the twisting, frozen trail. It seemed the mountain would ascend into the very heavens before we reached the top. Then, after climbing for another thirty minutes, our radio began to squelch. Another message from recon. This time it came through crisp and clear.

"We can see the cabin," the trooper whispered. "Lights on, people inside, two doors—back and front."

"We copy," answered Meyers. "You'll have support in ten minutes."

"Ten-four." The voice still low.

Its windows glowing in the night, the cabin seemed close enough to touch as we climbed the last fifty yards and leveled out. We were surprised to see a pickup truck parked close by. The owner was either highly skilled at negotiating icy mountain passes or too drunk to care. In any event, the truck meant at least one, or perhaps several additional people were inside. And the possibility loomed that we could be vastly outnumbered.

We huddled together and made final plans to storm the building. Confident we hadn't been seen, the advantage would be ours. Still we'd have to move fast with guns drawn and ready, the cabin a mere fifty feet away.

We were about to move in when Myers spotted something and signaled us to stop. He pointed with his hand. By the cabin door, a tiny red ember curved upward through the blackness. Seeming to appear from out of nowhere, it floated in midair, glowing brighter and brighter before arcing downward and out of sight.

A cigarette!

Someone dressed in dark clothing, all but invisible to us, was standing by the cabin with a cigarette cuffed in his hand. It seemed a miracle that he hadn't noticed us. We were close enough to hand him an ashtray. If he spotted us, the men inside would have plenty of time to react—perhaps with gunfire. And the cabin, acting as a barricade, would lend them superior positioning.

We held fast. Waiting. Crouching in the dark like leopards ready to pounce.

After several minutes, the shadowy figure took a long pull on his cigarette and hurled the butt into the snow. He opened the door to step inside, the cabin's interior lights flooding the frozen landscape. We ducked instinctively.

A barrel-chested man blocked his path. He stood in the doorway looking our way.

"Any sign of him?" His voice gruff.

"Nope."

"Good!"

They disappeared into the cabin. The door closing tightly behind them.

We stormed forward, boots crushing through the frozen snow. Reaching the cabin in seconds, we split up, one squad taking the front while the other advanced to the rear. A uniformed trooper, one step ahead of me, charged through the back door. I followed him inside and quickly sidestepped, our guns pointed in defense. *"Police!"* we cried. "Put your hands in the air!"

Four men stood with their mouths agape as officers poured into the cabin. I scanned the interior for additional suspects while two troopers broke off and searched adjacent rooms.

No one spoke. The men stared back at us with stunned faces. In seconds, the troopers reappeared from the back rooms. "All clear."

We frisked each suspect for weapons and IDs. Drago had a large hunting knife sheathed on his belt. I took it from him.

"What's this all about?" he demanded.

Corporal Meyers told him about the man who had walked into the barracks alleging a homicide at their cabin.

Drago shook his head defiantly. He was a huge man with fierce shoulder-length hair and a great flowing beard. "You think somebody was killed in *my* cabin!" he boomed. "Who?"

Meyers told him about our witness: how he'd watched a man named Lennie June being stabbed after an argument over drug money; how he took off running through the snow, only to be chased down by an armed man in an ATV; and that he was found the next day at the base of the mountain with a head injury, suffering badly from hypothermia.

A second man spoke, "Wait a minute!" His voice bitterly defensive. "*I'm* Lennie June! That's my truck parked outside. I got here two hours ago; the engine's probably still warm. I was in Philly all week, not here." He shook his head in bewilderment. "Man, this is nuts!"

Tension eased as he handed Corporal Meyers his driver's license. "There's my picture. Do I look dead to you?"

The trooper examined his license. Sure enough, the man who was supposed to have been murdered was standing right in front of us. "Something happened here," insisted Myers. "Nobody bails out of a warm cabin in the dead of winter and runs down a mountain in street clothes without reason. The man almost froze to death! Somebody better start explaining what went on here last night."

"I think he has mental problems," declared Slater. "Maybe the beer helped—he drank a whole case by himself. The rest of us hardly touched any. I mean, I can't believe this guy! I bring him up here to cool off and he pulls this stunt!" He shook his head reflectively. "He's been having trouble at home. I thought some time away would do him good."

"He's right," Drago cut in. "This is my cabin. We were trying to help the guy. He passed out on the couch, and when he came to, he started screaming some nonsense about

34

Lennie being dead. Then he ran out the door. He didn't even have a coat!"

"I went after him all right," Slater cut in. "But I didn't have a gun. I was trying to help him. He was screaming like a banshee when he took off. I hopped on the four-wheeler and looked all over for him. Couldn't find him, though."

Drago waved his hand suggestively. "Look around," he said. "Every gun in the cabin is locked up and empty with the action open. The ammo's locked up too. We did that to protect ourselves. We were afraid he'd come back and start shooting people."

The men were convincing, but then, so had been our witness. We searched the cabin and found nothing to indicate a homicide had taken place. There was no bloody carpet as our witness had alleged—the floors were bare wood. And the man supposedly murdered stood before us. We had no choice but to terminate the investigation and vacate the premises.

As we journeyed back down the mountain there was a general sense of relief that our raid had come off without incident. But Corporal Meyers wasn't completely satisfied. There was the nagging issue of the rug. Perhaps it was buried in the snow somewhere, a body wrapped inside. It had been too dark to see much of anything outside the cabin walls.

"We're going back up at daylight to search the grounds," he announced to his men. "We can't be certain of anything until we do."

It was three o'clock in the morning when we parted company, and the troopers would soon return to scour the mountain for evidence that a murder had taken place.

As for me, the first hours of buck season were close at hand, and my day was just beginning . . .

(Author's note: A search by a PSP helicopter and ground troops was conducted later that day. Neither a bloody rug nor evidence of a body were ever found on the mountain.)

Jocko and Jasper

WHEN HIS TRUSTY COONHOUND started to bawl, Johnny Midnight got up from the kitchen table and peered out a frosted window. Two hunters were crossing his distant snowfields. He watched them until they vanished into the woods, then he turned with a shrug of hopelessness and sat down to finish his breakfast.

But later that morning, as he steered out of his driveway on his way to work, he spotted the hunters for a second time. They were dragging a deer carcass across his neighbor's property, just yards from the highway. He parked along the berm and stepped out to confront them.

The two hunters stood woodenly as he approached. The younger, a scrawny teenager with shoulder-length hair and frightened eyes, stayed back. The other began to walk confidently toward him. A man in his forties, he was an amiable looking fellow with smiling eyes and a strong square jaw. He cradled a Remington rifle across his arms with the easy comfort of a lifelong hunter.

"Who gave you permission to hunt here?" demanded Johnny Midnight.

"Sorry, mister," said the square-jawed man. "I didn't know we were on your land."

"You're on my neighbor's property," replied Midnight. We usually don't let anyone hunt around here. Too many houses."

The hunter shrugged indifferently. "We didn't kill this deer near any houses. We got it a half-mile from here, up on Trader Hill. It's just easier to bring it down this way, that's all. Didn't mean to trespass."

Suddenly Midnight heard a vehicle churning through the snow behind him. He turned. A beat-up blue Chevy pulled

36

onto the berm and stopped. The driver was in his mid twenties with curly blonde hair that dangled to his shoulders from under a soiled ball cap. He got out and walked to the trunk and opened it. Then he leaned back against the car and examined Midnight with a cool, predatory gaze.

"About time, son," said the square-jawed man.

"Sorry, Pop. Battery's dead. Had to jump-start her again."

Midnight watched the older man's face begin to harden, his fingers drawing taut against the rifle, and he was struck with the icy realization that things were about to get real bad. The kid at the car was Jasper Hood. The hunter he'd just confronted was his father, Jocko. The Hoods had a reputation: they weren't people you wanted to mess with.

Johnny Midnight glanced at the deer. The spikes over three inches long, an illegal kill. He peeked nervously at his watch and started walking away quickly. "Just don't let me catch you trespassing here again," he called over his shoulder. Then he jumped into his car and sped away.

Within minutes, Johnny Midnight reached his office down town. He scurried inside and called Game Commission headquarters, explaining what he had seen. A dispatcher radioed the incident to me, and I immediately proceeded to the Hood residence, managing to arrive just after Jasper pulled into his driveway. I parked my patrol car behind his vehicle to block him in and stepped out.

Jasper got out of his car when he spotted me in his rearview mirror. His face twitched nervously as I approached, hands covered with blood. I had arrested him two years ago for poaching, and his hunting license was still under revocation from that incident.

"Hello Jasper," I said.

"Officer Wasserman!" He raised both hands, fingers splayed in a gesture of submission. "I don't want to go to jail!"

"Who said anything about jail? I just want to ask you a few questions about a deer."

"What deer?"

"The one in your trunk, Jasper."

His head swiveled left and right as if expecting someone to sneak up and grab him from behind. "I'm on probation, man. I don't want no trouble. You're not gonna put me in jail, are you?"

"Relax, Jasper," I said. "I have no reason to put you in jail. Just show me the deer. If it's legal, everything will be okay."

Jasper stepped back and pressed his butt against the trunk of his Chevy. "I wasn't hunting. Honest," he said. "I can't even touch a gun while I'm on probation. Someone else killed the deer. I just put it in my trunk and took it to the highway for this guy. Then he came by later and got it."

Although I knew he was lying, I didn't want to let on that I suspected his father had killed the deer. Instead I allowed him to keep talking. A lot of valuable information can be obtained from a suspect trying to save his neck.

"What guy?" I asked playing along.

"I don't know who he was," pleaded Jasper. "I just met him today. He was standing along the old township road behind my house with a dead deer. He asked me to take it to the highway for him and wait there until he came back to get it with his truck."

I shook my head wearily, "Jasper, you gave me the same story when I arrested you two years ago, remember . . . the deer without the head? Someone you just met supposedly killed it and ran off; you didn't know who he was or where he went; you were just an innocent victim . . . but there was this little problem, Jasper. A little problem called blood. It was all over your hands, just like right now."

Jasper fell mute, his eyes darting about like a cornered weasel.

"I want you to open your trunk," I said. "You can cooperate, or I can get a search warrant."

"But I don't want to go to jail."

I stepped closer. "Open your trunk, Jasper."

Jasper rubbed his hands up and down his legs and eyed me nervously. "Okay. I'll do it. I'll cooperate, if that's what you want." He pushed his butt off the Chevy, dug a key from his pocket, and opened the trunk.

"No deer. See? The guy took it, just like I told you."

The deer was gone all right, but the trunk was covered with fresh blood and deer hair.

"Tell me where the deer is or I get a search warrant for your house," I said. "It's that simple. The choice is yours."

"Okay, okay. No need to get legal with me, man. I could make a phone call. Maybe the guy will bring it over. My grandpa has a phone; he lives over there." Jasper pointed toward an old two-story farmhouse a stone's thrown away.

We walked over. The house was modest and well kept. No one was home. A phone hung on the wall by the fridge. I watched curiously while Jasper dialed a bogus number and shifted from foot to foot with the receiver pushed to his ear. After a few seconds he hung up and turned to me with a feigned shrug of despair. "No answer."

I chuckled inside. "Jasper, you told me you don't know who took the deer, that the man was a stranger, so how could you possibly know his phone number?"

Jasper swallowed hard. His charade was slowly starting to unravel. Time for plan B. "Okay," he said with a phony sigh of exasperation. "It was my wife. She killed it. I was just trying to protect her, man."

"Where is she?" I asked.

"At my house."

"Let's go see her."

"Now, you mean?"

"Yes, Jasper," I answered patiently. "Right now."

Jasper's two-year-old daughter greeted us with a toothless smile as she bounced happily on her mother's lap at the kitchen table. Jasper stood nervously by.

"Go ahead, Katie: tell him how you shot the deer."

Katie Hood, a fair and slender blonde, looked up at me with an uneasy smile. "That's right, officer," she said. "I shot the deer this morning while Jasper watched our daughter."

"Mind if I ask you a few questions?"

She pulled her child close to her chest. "I guess not. Are we in some kind of trouble?"

"I hope not," I said, pulling a notepad and pen from my pocket. "What kind of gun did you use?"

"A shotgun."

"What gauge?"

"I don't know. It's Jasper's gun, not mine!"

"Were you using rifled slugs or buckshot?"

She glanced nervously at Jasper. "Um, buckshot . . . I think."

"Where did you hit the deer?"

Her eyes went to the ceiling as she thought for a moment. "It was in the front. Behind the shoulder. That's the best place to hit one, you know."

I smiled and nodded in agreement. "Do you have a doe license, ma'am?"

Katie Hood's eyes flashed toward her husband and back to me. "No, I don't. Are you going to arrest me?"

Jasper suddenly broke in. "Wanna see the deer?" he blurted. "You said you wanted to see it. I'll take you to it right now." He cracked open the front door and urged me out of the house. "It's just a little ways from here, in the garage. C'mon, I'll show you."

"Yes, Jasper," I said. "I want to see the deer. That's what I've been telling you all along."

"I know, I know. You're right. My fault. Let's just get this over with, okay?"

Jasper and I walked along a common driveway that led from his trailer to a two-story house and a detached garage a short distance away. I followed him into the open garage and watched as he squeezed behind a tall antique dresser along the back wall. He lifted a cardboard box from the floor, set it on the dresser, and opened it. Inside was the head and hide of a freshly killed spike buck.

"That would be a legal deer if buck season was open," I said. "Whose garage is this?"

"My pop's."

"Where is he?"

"What do you want *him* for? Katie shot the deer."

I ignored his comment and pulled the hide from the box. A single hole from a small caliber bullet had penetrated the right front shoulder. *At least Katie got that part right*, I thought—

There was the scrape of a boot from behind. I turned as a man and a teenage boy stepped into the garage. I dropped the head and hide back into the box. "State Game Commission," I said, focusing on the elder. "Who are you?"

"Jocko Hood. I own this place." He ruffled the teenager's hair with his hand. "This here is Billy Black. What's your business, warden? Is Jasper in some kind of trouble?"

"He might be," I said. I could see traces of dried blood on the hands of both Jocko and Billy. I nodded toward the cardboard box. "Who killed the deer?"

Jocko shrugged indifferently. "I don't know anything about that deer. Better take that up with Jasper. I got nothing to do with any of this and neither does Billy."

"I don't think you understand," I said. "The deer is your problem as much as it is Jasper's."

"What do you mean?"

"The head and hide are in your garage. That means you're involved whether you want to be or not."

"How's that? I never touched it!"

"It's contraband," I explained. "The same as if you had a stolen car in your garage. You're just as liable for a fine as the person who killed it."

"That's crazy!"

"No. It's the law, actually. But I'm not looking to arrest everybody in this room. Just the person who killed the deer."

"But Katie killed the deer!" Jasper cut in. "She already told you!"

For an instant, Jocko looked surprised—he hadn't known about Katie's phony confession. But he quickly recovered.

"That's right!" he said, sounding relieved. "It was Katie. We were just looking to protect her, that's all. Can't blame us for trying to protect a woman, now, can you officer?"

"Sounds more like you're trying to implicate her rather than protect her," I said.

Jocko scratched the back of his head. "You saying she didn't do it?"

"That's right."

He shrugged a lazy shoulder. "Think whatever you want. I'll tell you what: you want to arrest me and Billy, go right ahead. Otherwise, I got nothing else to say." He turned and started back toward his house. Billy followed close at his heels.

"Can I go now?" whined Jasper. "You got the deer and a confession from Katie. Ain't that enough?"

"All I have is the head and hide," I said. "What happened to the rest of it?"

Jasper's eyes darted frantically about the garage. They settled on the back door. It had been left open, and I saw a maze of human footprints in the snow just outside. "Follow me," I said, moving for a closer look.

I walked outside and sidestepped a child's plastic swimming pool lying on the snow directly in front of the doorway. I thought nothing of it—just one more addition to the swell of odds and ends scattered about the property. Besides, something more interesting had caught my eye: something had been wrapped in a white bed sheet by the garage wall. It had been hastily covered with snow in an effort to conceal it. I stepped over and pulled it open. Inside were the hindquarters, front shoulders, and back-straps from several deer.

I looked over my shoulder at Jasper. "Who does all this belong to?"

He stared at the bloody deer parts as if they were severed human heads. His mouth fell open, but he seemed momentarily unable to speak, which only made matters worse. For it was then that I heard a series of faint, metallic smacks coming from the plastic swimming pool. I glanced toward the sound. Staring in disbelief, I watched as droplets of blood fell from the garage roof and splattered into the empty pool in bright crimson blooms.

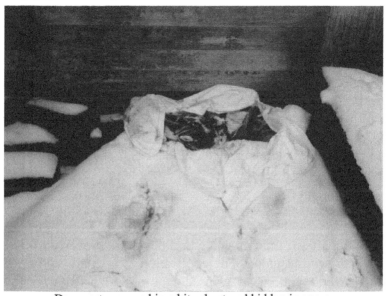

Deer parts covered in white sheet and hidden in snow.

I walked out into the snow-covered yard and turned to view the rooftop where dozens of butchered deer parts had been scattered about. There were front shoulders, hindquarters, backstraps, and what looked like at least a half dozen or more deer hides up there.

My eyes fell on Jasper. He stood by the garage door looking pale with apprehension. "Jasper," I warned, "don't make things worse than they already are; tell me what's going on here."

He nodded stiffly. "I don't want to go to jail!"

"I can try to keep you out of jail, but you'll have to cooperate with me."

"Yes, sir."

"Who is responsible for all this?"

"My pop and Billy. They threw 'em up there while you were in the house with me and Katie. I guess I brought you back to the garage before they could finish."

"Whose deer are they?"

"I don't know about all of them. One is mine and one is my pop's. We got them yesterday."

"Do you have a hunting license?"

"No."

I kicked the plastic pool aside. It skittered crazily, the snow under it packed with blood and footprints. I could see where Jocko had taken the deer parts out the doorway and dropped them into a hasty pile while Billy Black carried everything to the roof by ladder. The child's swimming pool had been ingeniously placed in a frantic, last-minute attempt to cover everything up.

"Bring the ladder from the garage and start climbing," I said to Jasper. "I want everything down here."

To proceed any further required a search warrant. I radioed for a deputy to come by and guard the Hood property while I went to see the judge. The application is a lengthy process, and several hours had elapsed before I returned with the warrant. When I entered Jocko's house, he and Billy were long gone, their tracks leading from the back door into the snowfields before disappearing into the woods.

Jasper followed close behind as I started my search. I stepped into the kitchen where a large upright freezer stood invitingly. Opening the door, I found the shelves packed with various cuts of deer meat that had been carefully wrapped in white freezer paper. A black marker pen indicated the contents of each package. I removed them one by one dropping them into a cardboard box, until I came across a magnificent palomino trout almost two-feet long.

"Nice trout," I remarked.

Jasper grinned. "Caught it in White's Creek."

It was a trophy most anglers only dream about, a once-in-a-lifetime prize. And I suspected Jasper Hood didn't catch it legally. But unable to prove anything I returned it to the freezer, now barren save the single large fish.

After searching the remainder of Jocko's house for additional evidence, and finding nothing, I took the packages from his freezer, along with the deer meat from the garage, and lugged everything to my patrol car. As I started loading the confiscated venison into the back of my Blazer, Jasper walked over to me. "I know who turned us in," he said with an ugly edge in his voice. "Something is gonna happen to him."

I turned toward Jasper. He had my full attention.

"Nobody will be able to touch me either," he continued, "because I won't be the one who does it."

I was astonished that he told me this, and had no doubt that he was serious. "Let me clue you in on something," I said, stepping into his face. "You've just helped to incriminate yourself by making that statement. Retribution against a witness is a felony. If my informant so much as catches a cold you're going to jail—got it?"

"Whoa!" yelped Jasper. "Ha, ha. I was just joking around, man. Having a little fun. I know better than to mess around with anyone like that."

"Good," I grunted. "Now why don't you take a walk while I finish up here."

Jasper turned and shuffled back to his house while I began loading the confiscated venison into my vehicle. All toll, I counted twelve hides, nine backstraps, nine hindquarters, thirteen front shoulders, one large box of venison scraps, numerous assorted antlers, one head, and about forty pounds of packaged frozen deer meat. Markings on the venison wrappers showing the date of kill indicated that four separate deer had been in Jocko's freezer.

As I loaded the final packages of venison into my vehicle, a blue Jeep pulled into the driveway and parked by the garage. A young man got out and walked over to me. His face grave.

"What's going on?" he asked. His square jaw and blonde shoulder-length hair bore a strong resemblance to Jocko Hood.

"Who are you?" I said.

"I'm Cody Hood, and this is my dad's place."

"I'm Officer Wasserman." I opened the Blazer's tailgate. "These deer parts came from your father's house and garage. Anything belong to you?"

Cody Hood stepped close and peered into my vehicle. "Yep! One of the racks is mine. Got him in buck season. Some of the meat could be mine, too."

"Well, right now it's evidence and it stays put. I have a lot of sorting out to do."

Illegal deer parts discovered at Hood's residence.

"Guess my dad is in trouble, huh?"

"Looks like it."

"Did you take the trout too?"

"No. I left it be. Your brother's pretty lucky to catch a fish like that."

"I'll say! He caught it with his bare hands, too!" His face beamed with pride for his older brother. "Kicked it right out of the water and grabbed it while it was flopping around on the bank."—

"Whoa, young fella," I said quickly. "It's illegal to catch a trout that way. Jasper is in enough trouble already." I paused and gave the boy time to think. "Now, are you sure we're talking about the same fish?"

Cody offered a sheepish grin. "I guess it could've been another fish," he said awkwardly. "It happened last spring— too long ago to remember for sure."

"Okay," I said. "Then we'll forget about the trout for now." I had plenty on Jasper and Jocko without adding to their misery, and saw no sense in letting the teenager go on and perhaps risk a beating.

"Want to do me a favor, kid?" I asked, climbing into my patrol car.

"Yessir."

I wrote my phone number on a piece of paper and handed it to him. "Have your father call me tomorrow."

J ocko Hood telephoned me the following morning. I spoke with him briefly, asking if he'd agree to meet at the State Police barracks for an interview.

"Name the time; I'll be there."

I checked my watch. "How about one hour?"

"Fine with me. I took the day off work for this. Wanted to meet you, too."

I hung up. His tone had been soft-spoken and sincere, but I knew better than to fall for his masquerade of humility. I'd been hearing about Jocko's poaching exploits for over a decade. He was an expert marksman, a cunning poacher. I was sure he'd have plenty of excuses for the deer parts I had confiscated. I sat back for a moment, pondering over how I'd best interrogate him, when my telephone rang once more.

It was Johnny Midnight calling about his run-in with the Hoods, curious about how I'd made out. I filled him in.

"Sixteen deer!" he cried. "I knew they were up to no good, but what you're telling me is insane!"

"Some of the deer might be legal kills," I said. "I still haven't sorted it all out."

"You've got your work cut out for you with that bunch."

"I'm afraid you're right. Especially with Jocko, he's crafty as a cartload of monkeys."

Johnny Midnight barked a laugh into the phone. "That's one way of putting it. Look, if you need anything from me, don't be afraid to ask."

I paused for a moment. Then said, "Okay. I'm asking: I've arranged a meeting with Jocko in one hour . . ."

Jocko Hood was waiting in the lobby when I arrived at the state police barracks. I escorted him down a narrow hallway into the interview room. It was Spartan by design, consisting of four white walls, two folding chairs, and a single wooden desk. Under the desk, a heavy chain was bolted to the floor to accommodate shackled prisoners. A one-way observation window was situated on a wall to our right. It looked like a mirror from our side. I motioned for Jocko to sit at the desk, his back to the wall. I pulled a plain wooden chair from the corner and sat across from him.

"You realize you're not under arrest Mr. Hood," I said.

Jocko nodded soberly, indicating he understood. "I want to get this off my chest. What I did was wrong."

I took a small notebook from my pocket and set it on the desk. "I'm willing to listen to everything you say."

Jocko leaned toward me as if to divulge some grand and confidential news. "Okay, here's what really happened: Three of the deer you took are illegal. I admit that. Billy Black and I each shot a doe on the first day. We don't have licenses." Jocko paused for a moment, then heaved a sigh of despair. "Katie shot the spike yesterday, and she don't have a license either. Jasper just hauled it for her. He didn't do nothing wrong—can't afford to, he's on probation."

I scribbled a few notes in my pad and looked up. "We're talking about a lot more than three illegal deer."

"You think?"

"Counting left and right shoulders—assuming each set came from one animal—then adding the heads, hides, and the frozen venison, I took sixteen deer from your property yesterday. The limit is one per hunter. You just admitted that three deer are illegal, what about the other thirteen?"

I watched the corners of his mouth melt into a gentle, convincing smile and wondered how many people had been conned by his easygoing manner.

"Four were killed legally in buck season," he said. "Cody, Billy, Katie, and I each got one. And you really shouldn't count all the hides. I found some of them dumped along the road and brought them home so I could sell them."

There was a tap on the door. A state trooper peeked into the room. "Someone wants to talk to you."

I smiled knowingly at the trooper and stepped into the hallway. Johnny Midnight had been watching through the observation window all along. "Thanks for coming," I said.

"Glad to help."

"Is that the man you saw with the spike buck yesterday?"

"Yep. That's him all right."

I described the longhaired teenager I saw with Jocko in the garage. Midnight said the description fit the kid that he'd seen with Jocko and the deer. Then I asked if a woman had been with Jasper when he pulled up in his car. Midnight gave me his answer and I stepped back into the interview room.

"Jocko," I said, lowering myself on the chair in front of him, "there's something I want to be very sure about . . ."

"Anything at all, sir. I'm here to tell you the truth."

"How do you know that Katie shot the spike buck yesterday?"

"I heard the shot and walked back into the woods. Katie and Jasper were standing over a dead deer. Katie had the rifle in her hands. She told me she killed it."

"Rifle...? Katie told me she used a shotgun."

Jocko crossed his arms over his chest and paused in a frown of thought. "Come to think of it . . . you're right! She did have a shotgun—Jasper's twelve gauge."

"Then what happened?"

"I told them they shouldn't have done it and left them."

"That's odd," I said.

"What's odd?"

"That you would scold Jasper and Katie for killing an illegal deer after admitting you and Billy Black each did the same thing."

Jocko looked at me with a narrow eye.

Leaning forward I said, "You're lying, Jocko. There was an eyewitness in the hallway when I stepped out a moment ago. The only people with the deer were you, Billy Black, and Jasper—Katie had nothing to do with this, did she?"

Jocko dropped his gaze and shook his head in weary submission. "You're right. I can't do this any more," he said. "It just ain't worth it. This whole thing is my fault. I'm willing to pay the entire fine. How much is it?"

"You have to understand something, Jocko: just because you're willing to pay the fine doesn't mean Jasper, Billy, and Katie are getting off scot-free."

"But I don't want to bring any grief their way," he said. "I'm the one to blame; now they're in trouble too."

"I understand, Jocko. But it's too late. You should have thought about that a long time ago."

We parted company, and I filed a charges against everyone involved. In return, the Hoods hired an eccentric attorney, and the court battles raged. Jocko's trial lasted eight punishing hours, Katie's dragged on for six more. When the dust settled, all were convicted. Jocko's fines amounted to eight thousand dollars. A staggering sum in those days. Katie Hood was found guilty of false statements, and conspiracy. She was sentenced to pay fifteen hundred dollars in penalties. Billy Black pled guilty to hunting without a doe license, unlawfully killing a deer, and conspiracy, which carried an eleven hundred dollar fine. Jasper got off easy. Because he was on probation, a plea bargain was approved to avoid jail time He pled guilty to hunting while on revocation and was ordered to pay a one hundred dollar fine.

I continued to work as a game warden in Wyoming County for more than a decade after my run-in with the Hoods. But unlike previous years, where I'd receive numerous tips and complaints about them shooting game unlawfully, I never had a problem with any of them again.

Eyewitness

ALTHOUGH MORE THAN thirty years have passed, I remember well the young man with a hole in his chest big enough to swallow a glass marble. Shot by another hunter, he'd been left for dead along an icy back road.

Deputy Bud Kowalewski and I were patrolling a three-thousand-acre state park, and about to break for coffee, when we saw a ranger standing along the road, waving frantically. I stopped my vehicle and rolled down the window.

"There's a man shot up ahead!" the ranger cried. He pointed a gloved finger toward a narrow road leading into the brush. "He looks pretty bad!"

With a burgeoning deer herd growing out of control, a special hunt had been organized by park officials. Two hundred eager hunters had drawn lottery tickets allowing them to pursue deer. My job was to see that they obeyed state game laws and park regulations. Now, just a few hours after the opening bell, one of them had been shot.

I cut my steering wheel to the right and raced up the narrow dirt road. Within seconds we saw him. His body rigid, motionless. Dread surged into my chest as I opened my door into the bitter morning air and rushed to his side.

He lay on his back, a small hole through the front of his blaze-orange coat. Blood oozed from it fatefully. He was conscious, in his mid-twenties—his face ashen, panic-stricken. Breathing in shallow, rapid gasps, his eyes remained fixed toward the slate-gray sky.

I reached for my hand-held radio and called for an ambulance while Bud kneeled by the young man's side. "I'm a registered nurse," he said, his voice soft, consoling. "You're going to be okay. More help is coming, but until then I want to take a look at your wound." Bud reached down and began unsnapping the buttons of his coat. "Doesn't look so bad," he offered.

He glanced at me, his expression portraying his true feelings: It was bad, all right. But he didn't want the young man to know. Attitude is everything at a time like this. There was a perfectly round hole just below the man's left pectoral, his body deathly pale. Thick, purplish blood seeped from his wound and trickled into a small pool by his side. My chest tightened at the sight of it. *He could die right here!* I thought grimly.

A Vietnam War veteran, Bud knew a thing or two about emergency treatment for gunshot wounds. As a U.S. Army Combat Medic, he had once had the daunting task of saving lives in fierce combat conditions when not so much as a Band-Aid was available. While Bud tended the wound, I spoke confidently to the man in an attempt to calm him. He looked scared. I didn't want his heart pumping any faster; he had lost enough blood already. "Ambulance is on the way," I assured him. "You're gonna be fine."

More park rangers began to arrive, some waiting for orders, others simply curious about all the commotion. I asked if anyone knew who shot the man.

"Whoever did it was gone before we got here," a ranger said. He was the one who had flagged us down. "Must have panicked and took off. I stumbled into him by accident. Lucky I did, too, by the look of things."

I wanted desperately to question the injured man: who shot you? what did he look like? which way did he go? If we didn't soon get a description, he'd most likely escape. But it would have to wait. His breathing was too thin. Verbal communication would be extremely difficult, dangerous perhaps. Kneeling by his side, I gazed toward the distant woods and wondered if the shooter was still out there somewhere. Wondered too, if the hunter even knew he'd hit someone. Bullets can travel a long ways. The hole in his chest looked like it came from a thirty-caliber projectile, indicating a rifle or handgun, but it could also have come from a twelve-gauge shotgun loaded with buckshot. I wondered which it was.

I glanced down. The young man had been watching me absorbed in my thoughts as Bud taped a heavy bandage over his wound to prevent blood loss. I smiled reassuringly at him. "Everything is going to be okay," I said.

He gazed at me for a moment, then his eyes closed and reopened briefly, peacefully, in mute response—

His eyes...!

I crouched by him, leaning close. "I'm going to ask you some questions," I said. "If your answer is yes, blink your eyes once. If it's no, blink twice. Understand?"

The injured man blinked once. Then, watching his face soften with relief, I suddenly realized he had wanted to talk all along but simply couldn't find the strength.

"Did you see the person who shot you?" I asked.

Blink!

Yes! He answered yes. The wounded man was an eyewitness to his own shooting!

"Was he older?" I continued.

Blink, blink!

"Younger then . . . around your age? In his twenties?"

Blink!

I continued asking questions about the suspect until I was able to ascertain that he had a full beard and had been wearing a camouflage-orange vest and hat. Because most deer hunters dress in solid-orange clothing and are clean-shaven, my spirits brightened. The odds of catching up with a suspect had improved by a long shot.

I glanced up to see a uniformed figure approached along the field's edge. Game Warden Richard Feaster had been patrolling nearby when all the commotion started and had run into another witness. He'd spoken with him at length, learning that he'd seen a hunter standing sixty yards from our victim as he fired three shots at a deer before turning suddenly to run off in the opposite direction. Feaster searched the area where the hunter had been standing and found three spent shotgun shells, the red casings were marked WINCHESTER, 00 BUCKSHOT.

"Did he get a look at the man?" I asked.

Feaster shook his head. "He was too far away. Never knew anyone was shot. Just thought it was odd for someone to turn and run off like that."

I gave Feaster a description of the suspect "I'll head back to my vehicle and see if I can find him," he said, handing me a small evidence envelope. "Shells are inside."

In the distance, I could hear the high-pitched wail of emergency sirens. With them would come the paramedics and more police. Still crouched by his side, I looked into the wounded man's eyes and saw a remarkable change in his expression: one of hope and determination. "You're going to make it," I said to him. Then, standing to my feet, I added, "I'll find him. I promise."

The wounded man smiled weakly, then he slowly closed and opened one eye. His wink a gesture of grand confidence. And suddenly I realized I had made a pledge that might be impossible to keep. But the words had spilled from my lips without thinking.

It was too late to take them back . . .

As Deputy Bud Kowalewski and I patrolled the state park, I radioed park officials and had them close all paved exits, asking them to detain any vehicle transporting a hunter that fit the suspect's description. With only six accesses to the grounds, each guarded by rangers or state troopers, we felt certain that our suspect could not escape in a vehicle. But I was painfully aware that if he'd fled on foot there was a good chance he'd elude us.

"Think we'll find him?" asked Bud.

"Hard to say," I said. "He could be too scared to think clearly and might be hiding in the park. Otherwise, if he's over the fact that he shot and maybe killed somebody, he's probably long gone by now."

Our eyes met briefly. "What about that young man?" I asked. "Will he be okay?"

"I think he has a pretty good chance now that the paramedics are with him. Luckily, we're in a heavily populated area. Hospital is close by."

"All we have to do now is find the bearded man," I said.

The words had no sooner been spoken when Bud whipped his head to the right. "Hey! Look over there!"

A bearded hunter who looked to be in his mid twenties stood in the middle of a vacant parking lot. He glanced nervously about, as if searching for someone. But he was dressed in solid orange, not the mottled camouflage style supposedly worn by our suspect. We drove into the lot and walked over to meet him. "State game warden," I said. "Everything okay?"

"I'm just looking for my ride," he answered timidly. "His truck was parked right here when we left this morning. I was just about to quit and go home." He searched the parking lot with his eyes, as if the truck might magically appear out of thin air. "I don't know where he went!"

"Where who went?"

"My cousin. His truck's gone. Why would he leave without me?"

Sensing that either he or his cousin may have been involved in the shooting incident, I said, "Did you shoot at anything today?"

"Not me. But I saw someone shoot at a deer about a half hour ago." He pointed in the direction of the wounded man. "It was over that way."

"Can you give us a description of him?" asked Bud.

"He was too far away; I couldn't see him that well. I heard sirens, too. What happened?"

"Someone's been shot," I said flatly. "Let's see some identification."

He pulled out a wallet, thumbed past several credit cards, and handed me a driver's license.

I wrote his name and address on a notepad and asked to see his ammunition.

"I only have a few shells," he said nervously. He dug into a coat pocket. "They're not even mine! My cousin gave them to me." He handed me two red shotgun shells, both Winchester double O buckshot.

Bud ejected three more from his twelve-gauge, then he put the muzzle to his nose. He shook his head, indicating it hadn't been fired.

"What does your cousin look like?" I said.

"He's about my age, twenty-two. He has a beard, brown hair—wait a minute . . . is he in some kind of trouble?"

"What was he wearing today?"

"Full camo-orange. I've been looking all over for him." Then, with dawning horror, he blurted, "You think it's him! You're looking for him right now, aren't you?"

"Yes," I answered. "What's the make and color of his truck?"

"He drive's a Chevy pickup—a blue Silverado. I knew he was in trouble when his truck was gone and you wardens showed up. I just knew it!"

I unsnapped my hand-held and notified all units to be on the lookout for the suspected vehicle and to detain the driver. Almost immediately, a park ranger radioed back that they had him stopped. The suspect had driven up to a guarded exit only seconds after I called in a description of the truck. Bud and I jumped back into my patrol car and drove out to meet them.

After removing the suspect from his vehicle, we handcuffed and searched him. "What's going to happen to me?" he blubbered. "Am I going to jail?"

With his shotgun and hunting clothes hidden behind the seat, he'd been trying desperately to find a way to flee the park undetected. Concerned only for his own skin, he had left his cousin stranded in a remote parking lot after running away from someone he'd shot and left for dead.

I wanted to knock him to the ground with my fists. Instead, I pulled out a Miranda warning and read it to him, explaining that he had the right to an attorney and that anything he said could be used against him in a court of law.

He spilled his guts, admitting he fired three shots at a running deer, the third one striking a hunter concealed in the brush. He told how the man had screamed out, but instead of coming to his aid, he panicked and ran away.

I tried to understand how anyone could abandon another human being that had been shot and seriously wounded, someone in desperate need of help; but I could not, even when I allowed for the initial panic—the sudden, overwhelming terror that might cause someone to turn and run. After a minute or two, reality would have to kick in: *a man is lying helpless on the ground, and it's your fault! Go back! Go back!*

But all this sniveling coward could do was whimper like a baby when I put him in cuffs. He showed no remorse for the wounded man. Didn't even ask if he was okay. Sickened by his callous disregard for human life, I placed him in my patrol car and closed the door.

Because the offending hunter had fled the scene and failed to give aid to his victim, he received the maximum penalty allowed by law. After pleading guilty, his fines and legal fees soared into the thousands and included the loss of his hunting and trapping privileges for ten years. Of course, this didn't include the cost of any civil suit that may have followed.

As for the injured hunter, he suffered some liver damage but eventually recovered from his injury. Fortunately, he'd been far enough away so that the shot pattern had spread significantly by the time it reached him, allowing only a single lead pellet to strike him—the other eight missing completely.

Sonny and Sher

FROM THE SECOND STORY window, she saw two men inside a pickup truck as it cruised by her house. In the truck's bed lay the skinned body of a deer. She scurried down a long staircase and ran out the front door, hoping to catch her husband before he left for work.

She almost missed him. His car was just pulling away when he caught a glimpse of her in the rearview mirror. Realizing something was amiss, he stopped and backed up. When he reached her she opened the passenger door and jumped in. Breathless, she told him what she had seen.

Deer carcasses had been dumped along the road near their house in recent weeks, most with the hindquarters and backstraps cut away, the remainder left behind for scavenging crows and coyotes. Perhaps these were the men responsible.

The pickup was well ahead and out of sight as they pursued it down the winding mountain road, hoping to catch up before it disappeared forever. Then, in the distance, they saw it. The truck had stopped briefly and was pulling away from the berm. When they got to the same spot, they pulled over and looked. The bank dropped sharply to the river far below. The deer had been dumped here, its raw carcass sprawled upon the forest floor like so much garbage.

Thinking they were in the clear, the men pulled into a convenience store a few miles away and parked. But their pursuers were behind them in seconds. Seizing the opportunity, they closed in tightly, blocking them in with their car . . .

I was twenty miles away when the message came across my radio that two civilians had cornered some poachers and needed help. I picked up my mike and called for any deputy who might be in their vicinity. Gene Gaydos happened to be in the area. He arrived within minutes and secured the scene.

By the time I arrived, Deputy Gaydos had already collected blood and hair evidence from the truck's bed and had taken written statements from the two witnesses regarding the case. After he filled me in on what had taken place, I approached the couple and thanked them for getting involved. Beaming with satisfaction, they both assured me they'd testify in court if need be and then went on their way.

Turning, I walked over to the men in the truck. "What's the story with the deer?"

The driver said, "We just wanted to get rid of it because it smelled bad." He was the younger of the two, maybe seventeen at best. A brown ponytail dangled to his shoulders from under a camouflage ball cap. "Honest, man. I didn't think we'd get into trouble, deer season being open and all."

"Understood," I said. "What's your name, son?"

"Bobby."

"Which one of you shot the deer?"

"Sher did."

"Who . . . ?"

"Sherman," he replied with a side nod toward his partner. "We call him Sher—you know, like Sonny and Cher."

"Gotcha."

The young man's eyes softened now as he spoke, his voice pleading. "Officer, I don't even hunt. I just let Sher use my truck to get rid of the deer. I hope I'm not in trouble."

Because archery season was open, I wasn't so sure I had much of a case—dumping maybe, but certainly not poaching. I expected the deer had been hit with an arrow and ran off, and that recovering the carcass had taken a day or two, causing it to spoil. I turned to Sherman. He was in his early twenties and dressed in full camos. "When did you shoot the deer?"

"Last night." He motioned toward his friend. "But he didn't have anything to do with it."

Last night. Odd, I thought.

Thinking he'd misspoken, I said, "What time last night?"

"Oh, I'd say about seven o'clock."

I was stunned by matter-of-fact tone in his voice. Deer hunting is unlawful after sunset. Surely, he knew.

"It would have been pitch-black by then," I said.

"Yeah, but we had a spotlight," he answered coolly.

I couldn't believe this guy. He was telling me about a poaching incident as if we were discussing what he had for dinner last night.

Suppressing my amazement, I asked what he used to kill the deer.

"A rifle," he said. "A twenty-two."

"It's pretty hard to shoot a deer with a rifle while holding a spotlight," I pointed out. "Someone must've helped you."

"Sonny helped me," he said. "It was easy, too. He held the light while I shot the deer. Easy as pie!"

"Whose gun did you use?"

"Sonny's."

"Whose vehicle?"

"Sonny's. I don't drive. That's why I asked Bobby to help me dump the carcass."

"Where is Sonny right now?"

"At his house."

I turned to Bobby. "You lead, I'll follow."

Sonny lived two miles away on a rural dead-end road. The small wood-frame cottage set deep within a forest of maples and oaks. As we pulled into the driveway and parked, gentle plumes of gray smoke drifted lazily from the chimney.

I exited my vehicle and stepped up on the front porch. There was a large picture window there, and I could see directly into the house as a man hurried out the back door. I jumped off the porch and ran around to confront him.

"Sonny!" I called. "Stop!"

He froze, then slowly turned. A young man with eyes strangely tranquil, as if he'd been taking medication or some kind of narcotics perhaps. "I'm not Sonny," he said.

Suddenly the back door lurched open. I whipped around to face a man in his late teens who started walking toward me. I stepped back far enough to watch both men at the same time. "Hold it right there," I warned.

He stopped. "I'm Sonny," he said dully. "What do you want here?" He wore a black T-shirt and tattered denim pants. A mop of dense brown hair fell to his collar, his face dark and brooding.

"State game warden," I said. "I want to talk to you about the deer you helped kill."

He shrugged indifferently. "I don't know what you're talking about."

"Oh?" I said. "That's not what Sher tells me."

Sonny's eyes widened with the realization that he'd been ratted out. He gazed over my shoulder. Sherman stood stiffly while Gaydos accompanied him in the driveway below.

"If you think Sher and Bobby are going to take the whole rap for this, you're dead wrong," I told him. "I know you held the spotlight while Sherman shot the deer. I also know that the deer was killed with your twenty-two rifle."

I paused to give Sonny time to digest what I said. "Sher confessed to everything," I continued. "We have a written statement. It's over, Sonny."

He shook his head and blew out a sigh. "Okay. Now what?"

"Where is the rifle?"

"I don't have it."

"What do you mean, you don't have it?"

"I gave it to a friend."

"What friend?"

"I can't tell you that."

"Don't play games with me, Sonny," I cautioned. "I'm giving you a chance to cooperate. If you come clean with me there's a good chance that only you and Sherman will be prosecuted. If others are involved, this may be your chance to cut them a break."

Sonny considered his options for a moment. "It's buried in the leaves," he muttered, nodding toward the woods behind me. "C'mon, I'll show you."

After retrieving the rifle, I had Deputy Gaydos escort Sherman and Bobby up to us. They stood by as Sonny admitted that he shined the spotlight on the deer while Sherman shot it in the head. Then he told me they loaded the deer into his Chevy Blazer and transported it to his back yard where they skinned out the carcass and removed the entrails. There was a foul odor coming from the body cavity, so they decided to get rid of the carcass. "Don't know why it smelled so bad," said Sonny. "We didn't want it no more."

"Where are the entrails and the hide?" I asked.

Sonny shrugged. "Sher and a friend dumped them. Buzzard bait by now, I guess."

"What friend? I want a name," I said turning to Sherman.

Sherman's face wilted with dread. "What's gonna happen to him?" he pleaded.

"That depends on how well you cooperate."

He stared weakly at Sonny for a moment before finally giving me a name. "Let's go find the bag of goodies you dumped," I said. "Take Sonny's vehicle. I'll follow you."

After driving about a mile, Sonny parked by a driveway that led to a two-story home in the woods. Sherman jumped from the passenger side and glanced over at me, his face showing a sense of relief that the matter was coming to a close. Dashing into the briars, he trudged out lugging a plastic bag stretched taut and bulging.

I motioned him toward me. "Know what the fine is for dumping?"

Sherman stopped dead in his tracks, his head retracting sheepishly into his shoulders. I took the bag and hoisted it into the back of my truck. "You're looking at a three hundred dollar sack of guts, my friend. But we'll talk about that later. Let's go see where you killed the deer."

The poachers continued ahead while Gaydos and I followed close behind. After several miles they turned into the paved entrance of a large estate and parked. Both men exited Sonny's Blazer.

"This is where we did it," Sonny announced, pointing into the field. "It was standing there, looking right at us. I parked here in the driveway and shined the light while Sher shot it."

I stared out the windshield in utter disbelief. "They can't be serious!"

Gaydos shook his head in wonder. "Dumb and dumber. Amazing someone wasn't killed."

We slid out of my patrol car and approached the men.

"You were only fifty yards from a home, a stable, and a horse pasture," I said angrily. "They're all directly in the line of fire. You could have killed someone!"

Sonny stared at me for a long moment, then his gaze drifted away, only to return in a kind of freakish, cinematic slow motion, eyes flat and dark. "Gee. Guess we weren't thinking."

"Get back in your car and wait there," I told them.

Deputy Gaydos and I searched the area and managed to find a bullet casing from Sonny's rifle. We also discovered a small pool of dried blood in the field where the deer had been killed. After photographing the scene, we took a small blood sample from the kill site and drove back to the spot where they'd dumped the carcass. The deer, a doe, had been shot in the head with a twenty-two caliber bullet. Certain it would match Sonny's rifle, I dug out the slug with a pocketknife and dropped it into my pocket for ballistics.

Sonny and Sher were each charged with using an artificial light to kill a deer. Both pled guilty before a district judge and received the maximum six hundred dollar fine plus a mandatory three-year revocation of their hunting and trapping privileges.

Unlike most poachers I'd met that started out young in life, I never ran into Sonny and Sher after that. And from what I heard through the grapevine, their redemption had a lot more to do with intervention by their parents than it did with the fines they paid to the Game Commission.

Graveyard Shift

THE SEPTEMBER SUN had been warm all day, and now the evening breeze pleasantly mild. Half-light would do just fine, thought Tim as he pitched his second horseshoe. It arced heavily and landed with a hollow thud, missing the pin by a yard. Tim looked at his two sons and smiled. They would cream him once again. And that would be just fine. He was home with them now. His work schedule had kept him away for weeks, and he relished the opportunity to spend time with his family.

The boys were about to retrieve their father's horseshoes when they stopped suddenly and turned toward the narrow dirt road skirting their property.

They could hear the black sedan coming long before it stormed past them, the engine rumbling menacingly as it approached. And when the old Ford thundered by, they caught a glimpse of the two men inside, the driver with a can to his mouth.

Tim had seen them around before. They were trouble.

When he heard the engine simmer to a low, throbbing roll, his chest tightened. They had come to a stop. He motioned for his boys to get down. A band of deer would be grazing in the field opposite his house.. Always near dusk. You could count on it. He squatted, waiting for the inevitable gunshot and prayed he was wrong.

The rifle barked once, its echo resonating like thunder off the surrounding hills. Tim quickly ushered his children into the house and then sprinted down the dirt road toward the state highway. When he spotted the Ford, it was already pulling from the berm. He watched as it sped down the highway. In the field, fifty yards away, a deer lay thrashing in the grass. Tim ran to it, frantic with concern.

The fawn, barely four months old, lay dead. Shot through the head, it had suffered little. As Tim stared unbelievingly at its limp body, a deep and seething anger began to overtake him. Killed on his father's property, his family had watched it frolicking here for months.

Then, in the distance, the Ford's throaty rumble came back to him. Tim quickly hunkered down, watching as it doubled back. He wondered if he would soon meet them face to face. They had a gun, and the prospect of a confrontation sent his heart pounding with alarm.

He could see the driver as the car approached, he was staring into the field as he brought the sedan to a crawl. But Tim had flattened himself in the tall grass, and the sedan continued on. He watched as the Ford turned by his house and started back in the direction it had come, the engine's guttural hum gradually fading into the horizon.

They would return for the deer. Of this, he had no doubt. He quickly left the field. Once home, he would call the game warden and then collect his darkest clothes from the bedroom closet. The sun would soon set, the moonless night turning black as pitch.

Standing in the bedroom, Tim squirmed out of his T-shirt while his father listened to him explain what had happened.

"Why, those no good bums!" he roared. "You were right in the line of fire; you could have been killed! My *grandchildren* could have been killed!" His fists were clenched, slate-blue eyes cold and hard. "Come on, son, we'll ride out to the Peek and see if we can find them."

"Dad, they'll be back for the deer," said Tim as he stepped into a pair of faded jeans and buckled them up. "I'm going to hide out by the field and try to get a tag number."

"There'll be plenty of time for that," his father insisted. "I need you with me to identify these punks."

Tim knew his father was going to the bar, with or without him. He wasn't about to let him face down two armed poachers alone. "Okay, you win," he said. "But if the car isn't there, we come back home immediately. Deal?"

His father nodded stiffly. "Deal."

The Peek Inn was the only tavern within miles. On any given night, dozens of locals could be found patronizing the place. The poachers had headed in that direction, and Tim's father hoped he'd find the them there. A former heavyweight boxing champion and knockout artist in the Marine Corps, he intended to make short work of both men—and anyone else who stood in his way. Although in his fifties, he still worked the heavy bag regularly, and his fists were granite.

The parking lot was packed when they pulled in. Although it had turned dark, the place was well lit by two tall lampposts. It only took a minute to see that the poacher's car wasn't there—profoundly disappointing Tim's father.

"We gotta get home, Dad," urged Tim. "I know they'll be back for the deer."

"Okay, son. But I'm coming with you if you're gonna hide out and wait for them."

"No, you're not," insisted Tim. "I want you to stay home with Nancy and the kids. I'll be fine. It's dark as a mine shaft outside. They'll never see me."

Tim watched his father's jaw bunch into a tight knot.

"I'll be okay Dad, I promise. I need you at home. Please!"

The air had turned cool as he ran toward the chapel just across the state highway. The tiny country church stood alone, hemmed by a beaver pond to its rear and hayfields on each side. A small graveyard flanked the parking lot, it was the perfect place to lie in wait. The deer had been killed just across the road, directly in front of it.

Dressed in black, he started across the highway toward the church when he spotted the poacher's car parked along the berm. His heart leaped in his chest. Crouching like some huge metal beast, the Ford sat with its engine off a mere stone's throw away.

His eyes strained to see if anyone was in the car but it was too dark. Thinking the poachers were in the field with the deer, Tim hurried toward the vehicle hoping to get a license number before being spotted. He raced along the macadam on the balls of his feet so they wouldn't hear him. The idea that a bullet might come whizzing into his skull loomed like a freight train in the night. His scalp tightened as he neared the black sedan. His breathing tight and labored.

Suddenly a blaze of light burst into his face, the harsh glare blinding him. He froze, hands shielding his eyes.

He heard the big engine roar to life, the metallic grate of a transmission jammed into gear. Suddenly the car came plowing directly toward him. It seemed impossible!

His legs were dead weights as he turned away. He only had seconds before they would run him down. He dove frantically for the berm, landing hard on his chest and hands, and felt a warm blast of air gush past him as the Ford rocketed by, his stomach twisting into a sickening knot.

He whipped his head toward the fleeing vehicle.

The license plate! He must get the number!

A small bulb bathed the tag in a dull yellow glow.

As he lay in the highway with his heart pounding, a jittery finger etched the number into the gravel at the road's edge.

Seated in weary attendance at a local sportsman's club meeting, I saw Deputy Jeff Pierce step through the door and knew immediately that something was up. He walked over and whispered that he'd been dispatched to a poaching incident and that the informant was waiting at a remote cemetery in Wyoming County.

It's not often that a witness will meet personally with an officer; most times they phone in a complaint and refuse to leave so much as a callback number. Intrigued and somewhat energized by the prospect of interviewing a witness at some dark and distant graveyard, I excused myself from the conference and stepped into the cool night air with my deputy.

It was ten o'clock when we arrived at the cemetery. Tim briefed me on what had happened. But his expectations fell short when I explained that a license number alone might not be enough for an arrest. We needed more. A description of the men in the sedan would be essential to a successful prosecution unless the suspects openly confessed to their crime—unlikely inasmuch as they almost ran Tim into the pavement as they fled.

"Let's take a look at the deer," I said to him. "If we find a bullet in the carcass a ballistics test could match it to the poacher's gun. We'd have a much stronger case that way."

Tim's face exuded some relief with the news. "Follow me," he said. "I'll show you where the deer is."

We walked single-file through the damp field, our flashlights scanning the knee-high grass, when Tim suddenly came to an abrupt halt. "It's gone!" he cried. "They must have already had it in the car when they saw me coming."

"That's good," I declared.

Tim gave me a puzzled look. "Why do you say *that?*"

"Because now we have something that connects them directly to the deer. All we have to do is locate their car; it should have traces of blood in it, which will give us enough probable cause for a search warrant."

"So what's the next move?" asked Tim.

"We run their license number and go after them."

"When does that happen?"

"Right now."

The tag came back to a Ford sedan registered to a Mary Bludgeon. I wasn't surprised that the car was tied to a female. Many poachers I'd run into over the years operated from vehicles registered to their wives or girlfriends. Their driver's licenses were often suspended—usually for driving while intoxicated. Most were bums who refused to work, drank excessively, and had long criminal rap sheets.

Pierce and I were eager to head out to the address. We thought there was a good chance that the car would be there.

But after a twenty-five mile drive into Bradford County, we ran into trouble trying to locate the place, so I stopped at a convenience store and asked a female clerk about the street we were looking for, hoping she could direct us to it. Unfortunately, she could not. "I just moved here last month," she explained. "Sorry . . ."

This left us no choice but to search every street in the vicinity, hoping to locate the Ford. Unfortunately, we came up empty handed and decided to call it a night.

The following day, I returned to the town and went directly to the post office. Because it was located in a rural area, where everybody knows everyone's business, I felt confident that someone could tell me where my suspect lived. There was only one person in the building when I walked in; she was busily sorting envelopes and packages as I stepped up to the counter. "Morning, ma'am," I said. "I'm with the Pennsylvania Game Commission."

She smiled briefly and gave my uniform a quick once-over. "I can see that," she replied with a raised brow. "Can I help you?"

I gave her the name and address I'd been looking for and she informed me that the Bludgeons no longer lived in the area, adding that they had moved to an apartment in the neighboring county about three months ago.

"Did they leave a forwarding address?" I asked, expecting more bad news.

She scribbled on a piece of paper and handed it to me, a knowing twinkle in her eye. "This is where you'll find them these days," she said. "Better hurry; they probably won't be there for long."

It was mid morning, the sun promising another warm autumn day as I drove down the long, dusty lane toward my suspect's new address. I wondered if I'd find anyone home. It was a weekday; if Bludgeon had a job he'd probably be at work. But drawing closer to the apartment complex, I spotted a black Ford sedan parked by a corner unit. My pulse quickened as I pulled behind the vehicle and saw the tag. It was Bludgeon's car. And as my eyes scanned the trunk for traces of blood, I noticed a key projecting from the lock.

I stepped from my patrol car and kneeled by the Ford's trunk. Traces of dried blood speckled the paint, and a single tawny hair—the summer coat of a whitetail deer—was stuck to one of the crimson spatters. The overwhelming urge to turn the key and open the trunk was almost more than I could bear. It shone brightly in the sun's reflection, like a lucky coin begging my attention. But without a search warrant, anything I discovered would be inadmissible in court, and I would risk blowing the case.

I focused on the key once more and considered why it had been left: This wasn't a case of absent-mindedness by some run-of-the-mill distracted motorist. Oh, the key had been forgotten all right. It should have been removed when they'd returned last night. But the trunk key was also part of a plan: the fawn had been targeted intentionally. Unlike a full-grown whitetail weighing over a hundred pounds, a fawn could be hustled quickly from the field as each man grabbed a leg, swept it off the ground, and ran flat out to the vehicle. The jutting key would be waiting, a quick half-turn opening the trunk. Throw the fawn inside, slam the lid and you're off. The sinking feeling that they'd had been at this sort of thing as a regular routine began to weigh on me, and I wondered how many deer they had killed over the years.

I looked into the Ford's grimy windows. More than a dozen empty beer cans cluttered the interior. A basket-sized Styrofoam container sat on the back seat cradling the melted water from last night's ice pack. The poachers were likely intoxicated when they tried to run over my informant. No surprise there, I thought.

Suddenly something flashed at the corner of my eye! The sun reflecting it.

I glanced up. A window shade bobbed in the apartment.

Someone had been watching me.

I went to the front door and hammered at it, positioning my body off center away from the line of fire. I waited several long seconds. Again I pounded, the door rattling on its hinges from my fist.

Certain someone was home, I decided to call their bluff. I put my handheld radio to my face, pretending to get a call, then, turning abruptly, I strode to my patrol car and sped off. Once out of sight, I quickly circled the apartment complex and parked at the opposite end where I could observe the Ford undetected.

Not five minutes passed when a woman in her mid-thirties opened the front door and hustled toward the sedan. An attractive blonde, she wore a white knit blouse and tight denim jeans. Halfway to the car, she glanced up and spotted me. Her face panicked. She scurried to the Ford and jumped in, the sedan's engine cranking vigorously before thundering to life.

I had my car behind her in seconds, blocking her in. I quickly stepped out. "State Game Commission," I cried over the Ford's deafening engine. "Shut it down!"

She rolled down her window and squinted up at me, a dark scowl on her pretty face. "Get your butt out of my way mister," she said defiantly. "I have to get to work and you're not stopping me!"

I have to admit, I was more than surprised by her attitude. I was used to dealing with male violators, some of them pretty rough characters. But this was an attractive woman neatly dressed in trim work clothes, not some calloused poacher with a day's stubble on his chin.

"Your car has evidence of a crime," I said, my voice still raised over the sedan's engine. "You aren't taking it anywhere. I want you to shut off the engine and get out."

She clutched the steering wheel with both hands. "And what are you going to do if I don't?"

"Then I'll physically extract you from the vehicle," I warned. "I don't think you want that."

She gave me a long, cold look before shutting off the engine. Then she opened the door and slid out. "Just who in the hell are you, mister?"

"Ma'am, I've already identified myself. Your car was involved in a poaching incident last night—"

"No it wasn't!" she shouted, cutting me off. "I was home all night. I didn't even drive my car!"

"How about your husband?"

"He was here too!"

"I'd like to talk to him."

"You can't talk to him. He's at work." She glanced nervously at her apartment. "I'm going to call my lawyer!"

I chuckled inside. Why was it that every time I had a hostile encounter with some lowlife they would threaten to call their lawyer? As if they had an attorney on retainer just waiting to come to their rescue.

"I think that would be a good idea," I said, again calling her bluff. "You'll probably need a good attorney. This car is registered to you. I found fresh deer hair and blood on it. You could be looking at a pretty heavy fine."

"First, I'm going to call my husband at work."

"Where does he work?" I asked, hoping she would say.

"I won't tell you that."

"Well, then why don't you go ahead and call him. I'd like to talk to him, too."

Now her eyes dropped, her voice softening into an uneasy murmur. "Look, officer," she pleaded, "I just started a new job this week; I really need my car. You can't keep it here!"

I offered her a simple solution: "There's a key in the trunk of your car. Open it, and we'll settle things right now. You say your husband and you were both home last night and the car wasn't driven. Maybe I'm wrong. If I don't find evidence that a deer was inside, I'll leave, and you can go to work."

She turned abruptly and marched to trunk. She looked down at the key, then back at me. And for a moment I thought she was going to cooperate. Instead, she jerked the key out of the latch. "You may be able to keep the car, but you're not keeping the key!" she declared. Then she opened her purse and dropped it inside.

"Suit yourself," I said. "But I'm going to get a search warrant. You really should leave the key. I don't want to damage your trunk with a crowbar in order to open it."

She stared at me, mulling her options. Then she hitched her purse under her arm and stuck her chin in the air. "Whatever!" she huffed. "I'm leaving for work!"

Pivoting on her heels, she marched down the dusty lane under the blazing sun. I watched her go, thinking perhaps she would reconsider and turn back. But the woman kept on walking until she finally disappeared around a distant bend.

My only recourse was to obtain a search warrant, but I couldn't leave Bludgeon's car unguarded. I picked up my mike and radioed State Game Warden Chuck Arcovitch. Although the deer had been killed in my patrol zone, the ensuing investigation had led me into his district in Susquehanna County. His voice came back in seconds: "What do you have, Bill?"

After giving him a thumbnail sketch of the case, I said I needed a search warrant. He advised me that his neighboring officer, Don Burchell, was patrolling near the courthouse twenty miles north. While on his way over, he radioed Burchell, asking him to contact the district judge for a search warrant on both the Ford sedan and the suspect's apartment.

Arco arrived in short order. "I know this guy, Bill," he said, exiting his patrol car. "Name's Billy Bludgeon. Works in the stone quarries. He's a career poacher." We shook hands and I filled him in on the details.

"I'll bet his brother was with him last night," he said. "He's a nut. I wouldn't put it past him to run somebody down, especially if he'd been drinking. Billy is a roughneck, but he's not crazy like his brother."

"That's good," I said, "because for all I know he could be in the apartment right now with a gun in his hands."

"I doubt it. He's not the type. He'd probably be out here with a convoluted story about how the deer got in his trunk, hoping you'd give him a break on the fine."

"It's going to take time for Burchell to get a warrant," I said. "I have some coffee in the car. Might as well join me." I grabbed my thermos and two cups and we walked over to a shady maple to talk shop until Burchell arrived.

Two hours passed before we heard from him. After jumping a few legal hurdles, he'd finally managed to complete the necessary paperwork. He said he was on his way, warrant in hand.

I walked over to my patrol car and took a hanger from a rain jacket I had inside. "Maybe we can jimmy the door lock with this," I said, walking back to the Ford.

Arco was standing by the driver's door looking at me with a big smile on his face. "What?" I said. "Got a better idea?"

He grabbed the door and opened it. "It's unlocked, Bill. Both doors!"

Although Bludgeon's wife had managed to snatch the trunk key and run off with it, in her haste, she'd forgotten to lock her doors. I chuckled with relief.

Scanning the Ford's interior, my eyes soon riveted on the dished console between the bucket seats. Lying inside was a spent bullet casing. The math worked: Tim had told me that he only heard one shot when the fawn was killed. Poachers routinely shoot game from inside their vehicle, the empty shell ejecting back onto the floor to be retrieved as some kind of perverted souvenir.

I inspected the Ford's interior for more evidence. Among the litter of empty beer cans and assorted junk, a bloodstained plaid shirt lay in a heap on the passenger's seat. We photographed the shirt and the bullet casing, then bagged them for evidence and shifted our attention to the trunk.

"Must be a hand release in here somewhere," I said, groping under the dashboard

"I don't think so, Bill," said Arco. "The car is too old. Ford didn't have interior trunk releases in this model until later."

"Too bad," I said. "We better wait until Burchell gets here with a search warrant before we break into the trunk."

Arco nodded. Then he looked over my shoulder toward the highway. "Speak of the devil . . ."

Taking a screwdriver and hammer from the toolbox in my patrol car, I knelt down and pushed the tip into the trunk's lock. Holding the screwdriver steady with my left hand, I reared back and brought my hammer crashing down against the handle. Although I'd managed to dent the lock some, it was clear that one or two licks wouldn't be enough to break through. I continued to beat at the lock for another ten minutes or so before punching the cylinder through the trunk. I'd hoped that the lid would pop open like magic. It did not. And a gaping hole where the lock had been was all I had for my effort.

"Man, that is ugly!" exclaimed Burchell.

I stood and stared at the hole I'd created, sweat trickling down my back under the warm afternoon sun. "Told her to leave the key," I puffed. "She wouldn't listen."

"Coming through," said Arco from behind.

I stepped aside. He had a huge crowbar in his hand. "Time to get serious," he said. Then, wedging the crowbar under the lip of the trunk, he used his body to push down hard, the lid moaning and creaking under his weight as he worked the iron lever methodically up and down. After a minute or so, we heard a loud pop. Arco dropped his crowbar on the ground and smiled over his shoulder at us. "Hope we find something."

He raised the lid.

The interior was a jumble of old engine parts, empty cardboard boxes, fishing equipment, and assorted beer cans. But among the clutter we could see graphic evidence that a deer had been inside: A silhouette of matted hairs lay spread before us in clear and fierce relief, showing where the carcass had lain. To the left, we saw a pool of congealed blood from the fawn's head, to the right, a fresh pile of deer droppings. The blood still tacky and fresh, the hair light and auburn—a fawn's summer coat. I raised a camera to my face and began taking pictures. After finishing, I carefully bagged some of the hair and blood for evidence samples.

I glanced up at the apartment and frowned. "I hate the idea of breaking open the front door."

"Got that covered," said Arco. "While you were punching holes in Bludgeon's trunk, I put a call in for a retired deputy. He's a good friend. Happens to be a locksmith."

Inside, the apartment was as neat and clean as any I'd seen. We walked from the front door directly into the small kitchen. The appliances were all updated and appeared to be brand new. Unlike Bludgeon's car, which was littered with debris, the kitchen looked spick-and-span. No dirty dishes in the sink or crumbs on the counter. Not even a chair out of place. From the tiled kitchen floor, a plush beige carpet led into the living room and extended into the back bedrooms.

Everything would be searched.

I started with the refrigerator. Along with the common food items one would expect to find, I discovered a pot of venison stew ready to be heated for tonight's dinner. I took it out and set it on the kitchen table, then went back to check the freezer. Here I found more than a dozen wrapped packages of frozen meats. Most were common grocery items, but I also spotted a deer heart and some venison steaks covered in plastic wrap. I reached deep into the back and pulled them out.

Arcovitch and Burchell had gone through the house to search the other rooms for evidence. Arco soon stepped back into the kitchen with a satisfying smile. He had a pair of work boots in his hand. They had spatters of blood with deer hairs stuck to them. I added the footgear to my growing list of seized items.

Burchell strolled into the kitchen right behind him cradling a Remington rifle in his arms. He'd discovered it inside a bedroom closet. Certain the ballistics lab would match the rifle with the bullet casing we found in Bludgeon's Ford, we seized it as additional evidence.

Satisfied that I had enough to successfully prosecute Billy Bludgeon for poaching, I left a copy of the search warrant on the kitchen table along with a receipt listing everything we had taken from the car and the house. Then I locked the front door and we departed.

The following day, I received a frantic telephone call from Mary Bludgeon. She could explain everything, she said. Yes, there had been a deer in her trunk. Her husband had hit one with the car. No sense wasting good food, so he promptly pulled to the berm, lopped off the hindquarters, and transported the meat back to the apartment. That, she insisted, was how the hair and blood got into her trunk.

I told her that I didn't believe a word she said and that I would soon be filing charges against her for possession of an unlawfully killed deer.

"Against *me!*" she cried "What are you talking about? I didn't do anything!"

But she was dead wrong. Deer season was closed, fresh blood and hair had been discovered in a car registered to her, and I had an eyewitness—Tim, who'd nearly been run down—who could place the vehicle at the scene of the crime. But I was after Billy, not his wife, and hoped my threat to prosecute her would bring him around.

"Look, if you want to stay out of this, have your husband contact me," I told her. "This was no roadkill. Billy and another man killed the deer illegally. They shot it with the rifle we found in your house. We might be able to work out a deal if he cooperates."

Stunned by the indisputable facts I'd hurled her way, she fell mute. But I could almost hear the wheels in her brain clicking at the other end of the phone. Alibis and excuses weren't working. So now what? And like every outlaw I've ever known, she decided that her best defense would be a good offense.

"What about my carpets?" she cried. "You tracked mud all over them when you came into my house and now they're ruined! Who's gonna pay for that?"

"We haven't had rain for six weeks," I reminded her. "We're in the middle of a drought. We didn't get any mud on your carpets—"

"I don't care if it didn't rain for a year!" she shrieked. "I want new rugs!"

Click!

I decided to wait a few more days before filing charges against the Bludgeons, hoping I'd get another phone call leading to a confession. We had plenty of evidence—enough to convict both Billy and his wife. But it would take a lot of time and energy to prosecute the case. Court trials can be complicated, and they're never a sure bet. That's why many criminal cases are settled with plea bargains rather than dragged through an over-burdened court system.

But the fact that Billy's wife called with a phony story about the deer, rather than Billy himself, had me concerned. Like many violators I'd dealt with over the years, Billy Bludgeon was a scofflaw. He had no intention of contacting me. When the citations came in the mail, he'd ignore them. Eventually a warrant would be issued for his arrest and I'd have to go after him, find him at home one evening or pick him up at the stone quarry where he worked on occasion. I'd haul him in front of the judge and she'd send him to jail. Then his faithful wife would come along and bail him out. They'd make time-payments on the fine, eventually paying it off . . . unless they moved again, in which case I'd have to track them down once more and arrest Billy for failure to settle up.

This was the way of the outlaw. And it probably would have gone that course if someone hadn't caught Bludgeon dumping deer parts in the field by his apartment a few days later. They called the Game Commission, and Arcovitch went directly to Bludgeon's place and managed to catch him at home. Billy took him out to the field and dug up a ribcage and some leg bones, claiming they were from a deer that was killed on the highway in Wyoming County. Arco figured he was probably telling the truth since he was already in trouble for the deer in his trunk. He told him he'd be facing another fine, however, unless he could prove the bones came from a roadkill.

Billy assured him he could, so Arco contacted me by radio and arranged a meeting.

Bludgeon's Ford sedan was parked along the berm when I pulled up behind him. The trunk, still broken and mangled, had been tied down with a nylon cord. We were on a remote stretch of highway adjacent to the county fairgrounds. There was a large pool of dried blood and hair on the road next to his vehicle.

He climbed out of the car and strolled toward me. Five-feet-eight and a solid one hundred and seventy pounds, Bludgeon had a dense, sinewy build from the stone quarries he labored in each day. His arms, low and apelike, were heavily tattooed, hands huge and rugged.

I stood in full uniform and identified myself. Bludgeon nodded and then pointed a calloused finger at the highway. "That's the blood stain," he said in a gravelly voice. "That's where it was hit. It was a fresh kill, so I drug it over the bank and cut off the parts I wanted. He motioned me to follow him and we walked to the road's edge. In the grass, a few yards away, I saw the remains of a butchered doe.

"When you take a roadkilled deer, you're supposed to call the Game Commission and report it," I said.

Bludgeon shrugged. "I didn't know. Next time I'll call."

I nodded, knowing he wouldn't. "Your wife wants me to believe the fawn you had in your trunk was a road kill too."

Bludgeon shrugged and said nothing.

I reminded him that we had obtained considerable evidence from both his house and car, and that I had forwarded it to the U.S. Fish & Wildlife Forensics Laboratory in Oregon. I explained that with a DNA analysis, they would be able to match the blood found in the trunk to the blood we collected from the field where the deer had been shot—in effect, putting the animal right into his trunk, thereby proving possession. I also explained that his rifle and spent casing had been sent to the State Police Crime Lab for a ballistics analysis. I told Bludgeon that I intended to prosecute him and his wife as soon as the lab reports came back.

Bludgeon gazed at me with a narrow eye. "Look, we both know I did it. If I plead guilty, will you leave my wife out of this? She ain't no deer killer, man."

"Who was with you that night?" I said.

Bludgeon hesitated. "Just some guy I met at the bar. I don't even know his name. I had too much to drink and decided to let him drive. Maybe I shouldn't have because he almost ran over a guy after we picked up the deer."

It was the usual guy-I-just-met story. I expected no less. He'd never rat on his brother.

"Okay, Billy," I said. "Fair enough, one deer—one citation. As long as you plead guilty and pay off the fine, I'll keep your wife out of it."

Billy Bludgeon kept his word and pled guilty to killing a deer in closed season. He paid his five hundred dollar fine in full and received three years revocation of his hunting privileges.

I continued to get complaints about him for the remainder of my career. I also had a number of run-ins with other members of his large family. They managed to elude me far more than I care to admit. These are shrewd and practiced outlaws with generations of experience behind them.

Poaching remains a way of life for them to this day.

Lamar Rube

"**L**OOK OVER THERE! A bear!" cried Tom.

Lamar Rube whipped his head around as a large black bear suddenly materialized from the woods' edge. It stood phantomlike before them, seventy yards away. They'd been woodchuck hunting, and they were upwind, the soft summer breeze veering their scent from the bear's keen nose.

Nearby, a vast blueberry thicket bloomed. The ripening fruit had lured it from deep within the woods. The bear swung its heavy head toward the berries and advanced in an easy, lumbering gait as the men stared in silent awe.

When Lamar shouldered his rifle and squinted through its scope, Tom paid him little mind, thinking he merely wanted a better look at the bear, its heavy fur shimmering in the afternoon sun. But to his astonishment, Lamar suddenly fired a shot at the bear and it began to run.

Then a second shot rang out, so close they could hear the *thwack!* as the bullet flattened into its flesh. Tom stood frozen in disbelief as he watched the bear crumble to the ground. "Are you crazy!" he screamed at the top of his lungs.

The wounded bear struggled to its feet and started to sway from side to side as if drunk. Then it started moving laboriously, heading for the woods.

Lamar Rube never broke his stance. He fired twice more, and the bear fell to the ground in a lifeless heap.

"Are you're out of your mind?" shrieked Tom. He was glaring at Lamar, his knuckles wrapped tightly into fists. "You can't just shoot a bear like that for no reason!"

Rube stood woodenly, his expression one of genuine bewilderment. "Hey, wait a minute!" he protested. "I'm gonna share him with you. There's plenty of meat for both of us!"

"Share him!" Tom chuckled icily. "You've got to be kidding! No way I'm getting involved in this. I'm gonna call the state game warden."

"Hey, don't do that!" pleaded Rube. "You'll get me in trouble!"

"Exactly!" said Tom as he strode toward his pickup truck. "Only you got yourself in trouble, pal. I had nothing to do with it . . ."

It was my day off, the sun had just set, and I was about to head to the river for an evening of bass fishing when the phone rang. An agency dispatcher informed me that someone had shot a bear in the next county and was being detained by deputies. The officer in charge was on leave. Could I assist?

Such is the life of a game warden, where your plans can be put on hold at a moment's notice. In Pennsylvania, all conservation officers work out of their homes. As a result, we are often called out during off-duty hours. I told the dispatcher I was on my way, then I hung up the phone, jumped into a uniform, and took off in my patrol car. Along the way I stopped and picked up one of my deputies to assist me.

After traveling twenty miles to Sweet Valley, I spotted some uniformed deputies standing along the perimeter of a shabby wood-frame house. I pulled over and parked. Deputy Gene Weiner stood by his patrol car. He had someone in custody as I approached.

"What do we have?" I asked, eyeing the suspect.

"This is the guy who shot the bear," said Gene. He's from Alabama."

The poacher was barefooted, dressed in a black T-shirt and jeans. I could see heavy bloodstains on his clothing.

"Did you search him?"

"He's cuffed and clean!"

"Do we have a carcass?"

"Right behind the house."

We crossed a dirt road and trained our flashlights on the back yard. The body of a large bear lay sprawled upon the grass, its dim outline a mere silhouette in the gloom of night. It was a good-sized male, and as I stared at the carcass the violation hit me like a fist in the guts.

I returned to the suspect and placed him in my vehicle. Deputy Weiner briefed me on the case while Lamar Rube, now a prisoner of the law, stared distantly out the windshield.

Rube, unemployed and penniless, had only been in Pennsylvania for a few weeks and was living with his girlfriend and her grandmother. When the deputies arrived, he spotted Gene from an upstairs window and charged out the back door in an attempt to escape. But Gene had anticipated this maneuver and had Rube's house surrounded before he approached the door. The poacher didn't get far before being tackled and handcuffed. "He admitted shooting the bear," said Gene. "The only thing we haven't done is search the house for a gun."

I looked back at the house. Two women watched us from a second-story window. A large, barrel-chested dog stood menacingly between them, his front feet planted on the windowsill. Thick cords of drool hung from his jowls.

I opened the door of my patrol car and peered inside. Something fetid drifted my way, and I wondered if Rube ever bathed. "How about that dog," I said. "Can the women control him?"

"He's just an old bull dawg," said Rube. "He won't hurt nobody."

I glanced back over my shoulder. The dog must have weighed over a hundred pounds and had jaws big enough to snap a two-by-four in half. "Looks like he eats nails for breakfast."

"Probably could," agreed Rube.

"Do you have guns inside the house?"

Rube nodded. "Upstairs, in my room, a thirty-aught-six."

"Is that what you used to kill the bear?"

"Yep. You gonna confiscate it?"

"Yes. We need your permission to enter the house; otherwise, we'll get a search warrant."

"Just take it," he said. "I don't want no trouble." He paused for a moment. "You ain't gonna hurt my dawg, are you?"

I slid inside the car with Rube and closed the door. "Do you understand that you are under arrest?"

Rube stared out the windshield and nodded solemnly. His shaggy hair, full beard, and thick protruding forehead giving him the appearance of a modern-day Neanderthal. I advised him of his rights and asked if he was willing to talk.

"Sho' nuff, warden," he said in a loose southern drawl. "Y'all got me cold."

"Okay . . . easy question first: why did you kill the bear?"

The poacher eyed me curiously for a moment. Then he shrugged a heavy shoulder. "Seemed like the right thing to do at the time."

I stared at him in dumb amazement, wondering how a mind like his functioned in the modern world. "That's it?" I said. "You see a bear in midsummer and just shoot it? Why?"

The poacher turned his head away and gazed into the dark surround. And I couldn't help but think that although only Rube wore shackles, I too had become incarcerated—a prisoner of his irrational and unstable world as I sat alongside him.

Then, finally, as if my question had been absurdly foolish, he spelled it out for me: "First I was gonna skin him . . . then cook him . . . then eat him."

"Didn't it occur to you that bear season might be closed?"

Lamar Rube said nothing. He bowed his head and began counting bare toes. For the first time, I noticed Rube's clothes were damp, and that the foul odor emanating from his body wasn't the absence of good hygiene but the reek of a swamp. "How'd you get your clothes wet?" I asked.

Rube slowly raised his head, the full moon causing sharp glints of light to flicker in his hair and beard. "When that feller I was with went to call the law, I hid the bear in a swamp so nobody would see it. Then when it got dark, I went back for it. I put it in my girlfriend's car and brought it here, but you guys showed up before I could butcher it."

"Someone must have helped you, who?"

"Didn't need no help. Did it myself."

"That bear weighs over two hundred pounds," I scoffed. "You couldn't have done it alone."

"Sure I could. I rolled him. Rolled him right into the back seat of her car. She has a hatchback—plenty of room for a bear."

"Your girlfriend didn't mind having a dead bear in her back seat?"

Rube offered a roguish grin. "She would have if I told her about it. No way I was gonna do that."

I doubted his story. I had handled many bears before. Their stout, compact limbs and excessive bulk make them extremely difficult to move, and the carcass hangs up on every rock, log, and stump as you drag it through the woods. But I thought it was useless to question Rube any further; he wasn't about to tell me who helped him, so I had Deputy Weiner transport him to the local district judge while I went to the house for his gun.

Lamar's girlfriend and her elderly grandmother stared at me with wide owlish eyes when they opened the door. I identified myself, explained what had happened with the bear, and asked permission to search Lamar's room.

"Help yourself," grandmom replied in a raspy voice. "It's up the steps, first door on the left. And good riddance to that empty-headed lout—and everything else that's up there, too!"

"Where's the dog?" I asked.

"Locked in the basement," the old woman croaked. "Right where he belongs! You'd be doing me a favor if you took him too!"

"Appreciate that, ma'am, but it won't be necessary."

After having the woman sign a Consent to Search form, I went upstairs into Lamar's room. When I flicked the light switch I saw the tanned hide of a large bobcat tacked to the far wall in front of me. In Pennsylvania, bobcats must bear a tag from the state or nation of origin. Lamar's cat was untagged, and therefore contraband. To my left, the feet and tail feathers from a dozen wild turkeys were nailed to the wall above a rumpled single-frame bed. To my right were two wooden shelves, the top one displaying a sizeable collection of alligator feet and teeth, while the bottom shelf held four severed bobcat paws and the talons of a great horned owl. A vast collection of guns and knives were scattered about the room—all high-quality merchandise— along with an expensive collection of archery and re-loading equipment.

I walked downstairs with Lamar's thirty-aught-six rifle slung over my shoulder and an armload of illegal animal parts collected from his room. Rube's girlfriend was waiting at the foot of the steps. Tears streamed down her cheeks. "What's going to happen to Lamar?" she pleaded. "Where did those men take him?"

"To a judge to post bail."

She opened her purse, searching frantically before pulling out a few crumpled bills. "I have some money," she said thrusting her arm out. "How much will he need?"

"I don't know," I told her. "The fine for the bear is at least eight hundred. Then there's this stuff." I nodded at the confiscated animal parts in my arms. "There could be some Federal violations here: Lacey Act, endangered species; we have to look into it."

She looked stunned, her jaw dropping as if struck with a blow to the abdomen. "I have to go," she muttered nervously. "Where is he?"

I gave her the name of the judge. She snapped her purse shut and hurried toward the door.

Halfway there, she turned. "What if I don't have enough money . . . ?"

"He's from out of state," I said. "They'll put him in jail."

"Oh, please," she moaned. "Don't let them do that."

"I'm sorry ma'am . . . really," I said. "You're caught in the middle of this, and I can see you're upset. But I can't help you. Killing a bear out of season is a serious offense. Lamar got himself into some trouble here, and he's going to have to pay the consequences."

She spun on her heels and hustled out the door. I followed her to her car. She opened the door and sat heavily behind the steering wheel, the dome-light illuminating the interior as she paused to gaze through the windshield in contemplation. Behind her, the seats and floor were covered with grotesque bloodstains, as if some demented prankster had smeared a bucket of tomato sauce over everything. Oblivious to it, she reached out and closed her door. Then she started the engine, dropped her car into gear, and sped into the night.

Lamar Rube never did make bail. Instead he spent several weeks in the county jail until his girlfriend finally managed to scrape together enough money to get him out—paying his multi-thousand-dollar fine in full.

I never saw Lamar Rube after that day. But I heard he took his dog and his girl back to Alabama to live with him. I'm told he found more trouble there too. I'm not surprised.

Incident at Hickory Ridge

WHEN CLEM CALHOUN stepped out of the thicket, I'm not sure which of us was more surprised. But if I had to guess, I'd say it was probably Clem. The sight of two game wardens eyeing him suspiciously had a paralyzing effect on the man, and he was temporarily struck dumb.

Deputy Gene Gaydos and I had been edging along a narrow dirt road in my patrol car, hoping to catch him hunting from his baited treestand, when he almost committed suicide by walking out in front of us. Thing is, we didn't want him to know that we knew about his treestand. And Clem, well, he didn't want us to know that he'd helped poach a mess of deer, and that the carcasses had been stashed back in the woods along with his rifle.

Hoping we hadn't blown our chances of making a case against him, I played dumb.

"Afternoon," I said rolling down my window into the midday sun.

Clem stood frozen in his tracks. He was in his mid-sixties with gray hair that had been cropped short. His thick neck and broad shoulders conveyed the stern appearance of a military man. Although it was deer season, he wore blue jeans and a brown canvas coat rather than the orange hunting garb typical of the day.

"Hunting today?" I asked.

Clem leaned toward my vehicle, craning his neck, and stared at me. He opened his mouth to speak but uttered only a thin croaking sound. Then he swallowed hard and managed to find his voice. "No," he said. "I . . . I've just been out walking. I don't even have a gun!"

I smiled as if that made perfect sense to me. "Okay," I said. "Well, have a good day then." I started to pull away, then stopped and turned my head his way. "Deer season's open; you should get an orange coat if you're hiking—might get shot."

I eased my patrol car down the road, glancing back at him occasionally through my rearview mirror. Clem Calhoun stood still as a fencepost and stared at my vehicle until I cornered a distant curve and disappeared from view.

"Think he's on to us?" asked Gaydos.

"Hope not," I said steering off the gravel lane onto a macadam state road. I turned left, pushing the gas pedal to the floor as I accelerated up a mountain road that ran conveniently parallel with the dirt lane we'd just left. I watched for a place to pull over, hoping to find a spot where we could observe Calhoun's baited treestand.

Gaydos spotted a thin dirt road ahead on our right and pointed. "Right there, Bill!"

I stopped just past it and backed in. The tiny lane climbed upward for fifty yards and leveled out, providing a perfect lookout point. I parked and grabbed my binoculars. Three hundred yards below, I could see a large wooden platform resting upon the outstretched limbs of a massive oak. Calhoun's treestand. It loomed high above the surrounding terrain where most of the other trees and shrubs had been cut down and dragged into huge brush piles that dotted the landscape like teepees on a wilderness prairie.

I thumbed the dial on my binoculars, preparing to focus on Clem's treestand, when I spotted a gray pickup truck racing down the dirt road we had just left.

"That's Clem's truck," declared Gaydos. "Looks like he's leaving in a hurry."

I watched the pickup rip through a narrow cut in the forest below. A thick dust cloud billowed in its wake.

"Guess we blew it," I grunted. "He knows we're in the area now."

"Maybe not," said Gaydos. "He was on the road when we bumped into him. Good chance he was getting ready to leave anyway."

"Hope you're right. Let's hang tight for a while. See how things play out."

Minutes ticked away like hours when a sudden flash of orange near Calhoun's treestand caught my eye. It came from the dense brush bordering the road. A mere swatch of color.

What is it?

I looked into my binoculars once again.

A patch of orange appeared—then disappeared.

A survey flag perhaps . . . ?

The wind-rustled foliage made it difficult to zero in on the object. My eyes strained through the eyepiece for another minute. Then I spotted it again—more visible this time and closer to the ground, moving in an erratic, bobbing fashion.

A hat! It was an orange hat! And as I examined it closer, I picked out the form of the person wearing it. He was hunkered on his knees, bent over the carcass of a deer.

"Gene, I think we have a successful hunter down in the brush."

Deputy Gaydos shifted his weight and adjusted his seatbelt "Well, maybe we ought to drive on down there and congratulate the fellow."

"Definitely," I said.

I turned the ignition and dropped my Bronco into gear. In a matter of minutes we were cruising along the narrow dirt road past our suspect. The dense growth at the berm so thick it blocked my patrol car from his view. He never looked up.

We went another hundred yards and saw an opening in the brush to our left. I cut in and exited my vehicle, Gaydos right behind me.

We could see him hunched over a deer now. He paid no attention to us. Just kept working on the carcass, butchering it where it lay. Gaydos and I, both in full uniform, were within a few feet of him before he looked up.

He stood. A pleasant looking man in his late twenties, of medium height and build, his dense black hair peeked from under his orange ball cap. He wore a full beard but kept it neatly trimmed. His expression a blend of grim surprise and tempered uneasiness. Bloodied to his elbows, a large hook-bladed knife protruded from his right hand.

Deputy Gaydos and I spread the distance between us. "Put down your knife," commanded Gaydos, a steady palm on the butt of his holstered revolver.

The man dropped his blade immediately, eyes darting left and right. Behind him, a four-point buck—one tine short of legal—had been neatly skinned and quartered.

"Keep your hands where we can see them and tell me your name," I said.

"Johnnie. My name is Johnnie Ray—but I just found this deer; I didn't kill it. I didn't want to see it go to waste, that's all. I don't even have a gun!"

I raised a skeptical brow. "No gun, huh? Where did we hear that one before, Gene?"

Gaydos glanced at me, then fixed his gaze on Johnnie Ray. "Why, I think it was Clem Calhoun, Bill."

I nodded in agreement. "Do you know Clem, Johnnie?"

Johnnie Ray dropped his chin, reluctant to answer.

"How did you get here?" I asked.

"I walked."

"From where?"

"Forkston."

"That's five miles from here," I said. "Plan on walking back with all the deer meat in your pockets?"

He shrugged at me, eyes to the ground—

Suddenly Gaydos cried out. "Bill! Look behind you!"

I whipped my head around.

Seventy yards away, a figure in orange clothing crouched behind a tree, watching us.

Realizing he'd been spotted, he began to run, a rifle in his hands. He was on a narrow footpath that ascended a good half mile to the top of the mountain.

"Stop!" I shouted. *"State game warden!"* But he only moved faster now.

Racing to the foot of the mountain, I shouted again, commanding him to stop. He was gaining ground quickly. He'd soon be out of sight.

I started after him. My bulky winter uniform, heavy boots, and leather holster adding considerable weight and clumsiness to my stride. The slope, covered with damp leaves, made for some slippery footing. I ran as fast as I could, my feet digging feverishly into the loose soil.

There was blood now. The ground covered in red gore beneath my pounding boots. To my right, the entrails from two deer lay in separate piles.

Suddenly, I knew why he was running . . . why *I* was running!

I could see him up ahead. Less than a hundred feet separated us. His pace had slowed considerably. The climb becoming more steep. Hunched forward, he labored up the trail until he rounded a bend.

Then, all at once, he was gone!

I stopped to catch my breath. My heavy clothing coupled with the sharp climb made me feel like I just ran the Boston Marathon. I scanned the trail ahead, eyes straining to detect the slightest movement.

I was certain he'd removed his orange coat. Certain too, that he'd stopped running and had concealed himself somewhere.

Cautiously, I moved forward. My gun still holstered for fear of slipping on the unstable ground and fouling the barrel. I palmed its grip, ready to draw and fire if necessary.

The woods had opened wide here. There was no cover. I was an open target. My scalp tightened as I imagined my chest being ripped apart by some lunatic magnum slug. Then I quickly shook the nightmare out of my head, my skull screaming back at me that in thirty years of chasing armed poachers I had always come out unscathed.

I continued along the narrow footpath until I reached the first bench. Suddenly I saw him. Ten feet away, crouched low in the bushes, his back pressed tightly against the gnarled roots of a towering oak. His orange coat and rifle lay well out of reach.

And he was shaking with fear.

I stopped. Taken aback. He was only a boy!

"How old are you, son?"

"Four . . . four . . . teen, sir."

My mood softened. The kid was scared half to death. "You shouldn't run from the law, you know."

He stared up at me, eyes wide and searching. "You gonna take me to jail?"

"Not if you behave yourself." I picked up his rifle and opened the action. It was empty. "Put your coat on, son," I said, sweeping it off the ground and handing it to him. "You'll catch cold for sure."

He squirmed into the coat and buttoned it up. "I don't want to run anymore."

"Good," I said. "Because I'm too old to keep chasing you."

We started back down the mountain, walking slow, side by side.

"Does your mom and dad know you're hunting today?"

"No, sir. My mom thinks I'm in school."

I nodded reflectively. "Might have played hooky once or twice myself when I was your age."

The boy glanced at me and smiled. Then his expression quickly turned grave. "Guess I'm in trouble, huh?"

"Probably more with your mother than with me. Where do you live, son?"

"Forkston."

"Johnnie Ray bring you here?"

"Mr. Calhoun brought me. He brought Mr. Ray, too. We were all hunting today."

"Did Mr. Ray shoot the deer we found him with?"

"Yes sir."

"How do you know that?"

"I watched him shoot it. I watched him shoot a bunch more too."

When we reached the base of the mountain, Deputy Gaydos was standing there with Johnnie Ray. While I'd been gone, he'd discovered two plastic trash bags filled with deer parts near Clem's treestand. They were hidden inside a brush pile the size of a large automobile. Digging further into the maze, Gaydos also discovered two deer carcasses—both illegal does with their hindquarters and backstraps removed. Two high-powered rifles had been hidden along with them.

"Did you check all the brush piles, Gene?"

"One left," he said. "You got back before I had a chance."

I had Gaydos take the boy out of hearing range for a moment, then I turned to Johnnie Ray. He stood with his hands stuffed in his pockets, counting blades of grass.

"Want to tell me what really happened here?" I said.

He nodded solemnly. "The kid's my cousin. Guess he told you I shot the two deer that your deputy found."

"That's right."

"I killed the one by the road too. Clem was putting on a drive when they came out of the woods and stopped below my treestand—Clem's treestand, actually. He posted me up there while he pushed the woods." The poacher hesitated a moment and shook his head. "Couldn't resist. I shot all three of them. Shouldn't have . . . but I did."

"Is that it?" I said. "No more deer hidden anywhere?"

"That's it," he said. "You got them all."

A cold moistness touched my cheek. I looked up into a slate-gray sky. Snowflakes began to dance lazily to the ground. It was late, the day fading into night. There would be little time to check for more deer.

I asked Gaydos to gather the guns, carcasses, and bags of deer parts while I looked at the remaining brush pile. Johnnie Ray seemed all too happy to admit killing three deer, and I suspected there would be more. Dusk was descending quickly as my flashlight probed into a tangle of boney branches big enough to fill a two-car garage. It wasn't long before my light picked out the white belly of a fourth dead doe. I pried a snarl of branches out of my way and reached back into the mess until I could grab a hoof. When I pulled the doe toward me, I saw a second one right behind it.

Johnnie Ray stiffened when he saw me dragging the carcasses toward him. "Are you going to start telling the truth," I said, "or do we have to play around here all night?"

He raised both hands defensively. "I swear on my mother's grave, you got the last two. I killed one of 'em and Clem killed the other. Honest, sir. We only killed five deer."

I felt satisfied we had them all. Not that I believed Johnnie Ray, but rather that we had searched all the brush piles and there really wasn't any place else to look. "Where is Clem?" I demanded.

Johnnie shook his head. "I have no idea. He was supposed to come back for me an hour ago, but he never showed up."

Suddenly a pickup truck came roaring up the road toward us. Deputy Jeff Pierce. Gaydos had radioed out to him for assistance while I'd been chasing after the kid. We needed his truck to secure the more than six hundred pounds of illegal deer parts we had collected. As he rolled in, the snow started to fall in earnest, and the night began to envelop us.

Then, while we loaded the bulky carcasses and bags full of deer parts into the bed of Jeff's pickup, headlights appeared in the distance.

"I'll bet that's Clem Calhoun coming back for the deer," declared Gaydos.

"That's a bet I think you're going to win." I said. I hustled over to my patrol car and blocked the road, my red flashing lights signaling the vehicle to stop. It was risky to do this. I was an easy target if someone in the truck wanted to shoot me. But it was a chance I decided to take at the moment.

I approached the vehicle cautiously, directing the beam of my flashlight at the two silhouettes in the cab. Clem Calhoun sat in the passenger seat, while a much older man, well into his seventies, remained behind the steering wheel. Both suspects appeared to be in a state of mild shock as I approached their open window.

"You came back!" announced Clem. "Thought you'd be long gone by now."

"The five deer carcasses we found were enough to make me hang around for a while," I told him. "We know you were involved. We found both rifles, Clem. The boy, too. I want you to wait here until we get everyone in my patrol car. Then you and your friend can head over to the state police barracks. I'll be right behind you."

Clem nodded soberly and waited until my deputies took Johnnie Ray and the boy into custody. Then I signaled for them to go and followed their truck down the narrow dirt lane toward the state highway.

Wasserman and Gaydos with 600 pounds of confiscated deer parts.

"I had no idea that my son was with those two men," the woman declared. "He was supposed to be in school!"

We were standing in the lobby of the Pennsylvania State Police Barracks. Clem Calhoun and Johnnie Ray were in a back room waiting for me.

"Your son told me as much after I caught up with him," I said. "He was in some bad company today."

"Will there be any charges brought against him?"

"Not this time," I said. "I'm sure you'll come up with an appropriate punishment."

She looked down at her son and frowned. "Your father is waiting in the car. Go out and see him."

The boy scurried out the door without looking back.

"Thank you, officer," she said. "He won't be associating with those two ever again. I can promise you that."

"Yes, ma'am." I glanced at my watch. "They're waiting for me right now."

Turning to leave, she paused and looked back at me. "Watch out for Clem," she warned. "He's unstable."

I nodded at the dispatcher through his plate glass window and he pressed a buzzer indicating that the heavy door leading into the barracks was unlocked. I opened it and walked down a corridor into a room where I found my two suspects sitting with deputy Gaydos.

Both men signed written confessions implicating themselves in the unlawful killing and possession of five whitetail deer. Clem admitted he had just stepped out of the woods on his way to his truck when Gaydos and I came by. Instead of returning for Johnnie Ray and the deer parts as planned, Clem hightailed it back to his house. But curiosity had eventually gotten the best of him, and he decided to return only to stumble upon us once again.

I filed multiple citations against the two men. Both pled guilty rather than take a court trial, and they paid a combined total of five thousand dollars in fines plus court costs—the maximum penalty at the time. They also lost their hunting and trapping privileges for five years.

Thirty days later, the state police called me regarding a hunting related shooting incident on Clem Calhoun's property. A state trooper asked that I come by right away. The victim, a bow hunter, had just walked into the barracks. They would assist with the investigation if need be but wanted me to interview the man first.

When I walked into the Interrogation Room, a trooper was sitting with the victim, who appeared to be in his mid thirties. He looked white as a ghost. He was visibly shaken, even though the incident had taken place more than an hour ago. I sat across from him and took out a notepad and pen. "Are you injured in any way, sir?"

"Injured?" He barked a nervous chuckle. "Lucky I'm not dead!" His entire body convulsed with emotion. "The man is crazy! He could have killed me!"

"What man?"

"Clem Calhoun."

"You're certain?"

"I ought to be. He's my uncle."

His answer didn't surprise me. Over the years, I'd investigated more than a few hunting related shooting incidents where friends or relatives had shot family members who were either in the line of fire or mistaken for a turkey or deer. "Tell me what happened," I said.

He glanced nervously at the trooper and back to me. "I'm in a treestand on Clem's property, and it's getting dark, when I see Clem pull into his cabin and park behind my truck. I think nothing of it. He gets out and sees me up there. I'm in full camo, fifty yards away, right?—"

I nodded at him.

"—So he pulls out a handgun and yells, 'Get the hell out of my treestand!' Then he fires a warning shot at the moon!"

A tear tracked down the man's cheek. His voice cracked and ragged.

"So I start lowering my b . . . bow, ready to climb down, and he empties his gun at me! Five m . . . more shots. I can hear them hitting the branches all around me: *BAM-BAM-BAM-BAM-BAM!* One of 'em flies right puh . . . past my head! Sounds like, you know, a humming bird buzzing me it's so close. So I yell, *Don't shoot! It's me! It's me!* And he walks into his cabin and slams the door. That's when I got out of the tree and ran to my truck. I went straight to the police."

I looked at the trooper. "This is no hunting incident. Reckless endangerment, maybe. Or something more. But Clem wasn't hunting when he shot at this man. It doesn't fall into a violation of the Game and Wildlife Code."

The trooper looked at the victim. "You say the guy is your uncle. Does he have a vendetta against you?"

He shook his head. "He has a problem with his temper. I hardly know him, really. He has nothing against me."

"Do you think he's still at his camp?"

"He'll probably stay there all night. He usually does."

As our patrol cars approached Calhoun's cabin, we could see lights inside. We stopped on the road and exited our vehicles, but Clem Calhoun walked out the door before we reached his front porch. He stopped cold at the commanding sight of five uniformed officers and threw his arms in the air, palms open.

One of the troopers went to his patrol car and opened the back door. He said something to the victim inside. They were too far away for me to hear, but I saw the victim nod his head. "That's him," he mouthed.

Clem Calhoun was immediately handcuffed and placed under arrest. Two troopers escorted him to an awaiting patrol car and whisked him away. He'd soon be sleeping in the harsh confines of the county jail.

On my way home that night, I recalled how just weeks before, I had blocked the road with my patrol car and approached Calhoun and his companion as they sat inside the cab of a darkened truck. A cold shiver ran down my spine as I thought about his unpredictable mood swings and how close I might have come to being shot and killed.

And so I asked myself, would I do it again? I mean, approach a vehicle with a criminal suspect inside, not knowing what the outcome might be? And of course, I knew I would. It's what every police officer does in every vehicle stop they make. It comes with the territory. It's part of the job. And although we try to be as cautious as possible, the possibility remains that our suspect will be armed and ready to shoot. It's a risk we acknowledge, one that we must accept every single day that we step into a uniform.

Cemetery Road

THE TWO FIGURES edging toward his treestand puzzled him. He knew they'd seen him. And common decorum should have precluded any chance they'd intrude upon his location. After all, they were surrounded by two thousand acres of stately forest—ample range for even the most discriminate deer hunter.

But not all hunters prescribe to the customary rules of fair play. And these two happened to be elite members of that breed. Despite Dominic's obvious presence, both men took stands within his immediate shooting zone: one to his left, the other to his right.

It had been a long walk up the mountain: at least a mile, figured Dominic, and he wasn't about to be squeezed out by two ill-mannered intruders. This was prime deer country, and the season's opening hour was upon him. He'd just have to stick it out. His treestand gave him a distinct advantage over his two rivals on the ground, for he could see a deer coming from afar. They could not.

As dawn began to spread long fingers of light through the forest, Dominic's eyes searched for the slightest movement. The flash of a tail or the gentle bob of a head would put him on instant alert. He ranged his gaze over the horizon, gradually working back along the forest floor until he found himself scanning the ground directly below.

That's when his knees suddenly weakened.

He recognized the two forms at once. They had gone unnoticed in the predawn gloom. But now, with the morning light, they stood out plainly. A mere fifty feet away—one brown, one white.

Salt blocks? Here? What the . . . !

Suddenly he realized why the two mysterious hunters had set up so close to him. He also realized that he had inadvertently placed his treestand near their illegal bait. As a state trooper and retired deputy game warden, Dominic was outraged. But instead of confronting the men, he quietly packed his gear, descended from the tree, and hustled back down the mountain.

Both poachers nodded unsuspectingly as he passed them, unaware that they would soon be rewarded for their unsportsmanlike behavior.

Once out of sight, Dominic used his cell phone to contact me and set up a rendezvous along Cemetery Road.

It took him a good half-hour to hoof it down, about the same time it took Deputy Pierce and me to get there from the opposite end of the county where we'd been investigating another violation.

We arrived within minutes of each other.

"Bill!" cried Dominic as he stuck out a hand. "Great to see you again."

I grabbed his palm. "Good to see you too, Dominic. Sorry your hunt has been wrecked."

"No problem. I'll have other days to get a deer. So long as we nab these two; that's the only hunt I want right now."

A long and strenuous climb, we were moving slowly up the mountain when a shot suddenly rang out.

We froze in our tracks. "Wow! That was close!" I hissed.

Suddenly a doe came crashing from the woods. It stopped directly in front of us. Ice ran through my veins as I waited for a second bullet to come rocketing our way.

"DON'T SHOOT!" I hollered. "HUMANS! DO NOT SHOOT!"

A voice in the woods boomed out to us. "HELLO . . . ?"

The deer suddenly ran off, and as we watched it disappear into the trees, I called out to the hunter, signaling my approach. "State game warden! I'm coming toward you."

Confident my presence was known, I moved ahead, the hunter soon materializing among the trees. He sat on a stump in a depression, fifty yards away. Although we were wearing orange vests and hats, the hilly terrain had blocked us from his view—any one of us could have been killed. I told him we were heading up the mountain and that we would soon be returning, advising him that it was not safe to fire in that direction. He apologized for scaring the daylights out of us and quickly packed his gear, promising to seek higher ground where he'd have a better view of his surroundings.

We trekked ahead for another half hour before reaching a broad plateau. Although vast, the woods were open here, lending a clear visibility to the surroundings. Dominic stopped abruptly and pointed out the first hunter. He stood at the base of a tree a mere twenty yards away, his back toward us as he cradled a scoped rifle.

"The other one is just below him," whispered Dominic. "Can't see him from here, but I know where he's posted."

"I got this one," I said. "You and Jeff head over to his partner."

My suspect looked to be in his late fifties. He stiffened when he saw me coming and lowered the muzzle of his rifle to the ground. "Something wrong, officer?"

I stepped close. "You're hunting in a baited area."

He looked bewildered. "Where? I don't see any bait."

I reached out and took his rifle. "I'll explain more in a minute." I released the fully loaded clip into my hand and snapped the bolt action back, ejecting a live round. I pocketed it along with the clip. "Let's see your hunting license and some identification."

A non-resident from New Jersey, he had proper ID and a legal hunting license. "Are you with anybody today?" I asked, knowing, of course, that he was.

"Yes, my son," he said, pointing. "He's over there, talking to the other wardens."

Dominic and Pierce were standing twenty-five yards below us, questioning him. "Okay," I said. "Walk on down, I'll follow."

His son was in his mid-twenties. A giant of a man, he knelt by a medium-sized doe, dwarfing it. A drag-rope had been secured to its neck. Nearby, two twelve-inch salt blocks lay on the ground. He looked up at me as I approached and I watched him focus on the metal nametag pinned to my chest. His eyes widened. "Officer Wasserman!"

"Have we met before?"

"Not exactly, sir. But I have two of your books."

His comment caught me off guard. All my writings have been testaments against poaching, and I questioned his rationale.

"Well, then, why are you doing *this?*" I said flatly.

He shrugged and looked away, then stood to his feet. He was huge, perhaps three hundred pounds or more, not much of it fat. "Sir, my father didn't know about the salt blocks. I brought them up here two months ago—never told him about it. This is all my fault. Just tell me what the fine is. I'm guilty. I'll pay."

Before I could respond, my hand-held radio blurted a message about another baiting incident several miles away. The dispatcher stated that the informant wanted to meet me as soon as possible but refused to provide any additional information except that his name was Jay.

Jay was a code name. I knew the man. A confidential informant, he'd often given me good information in the past. I thumbed the transmit button on my portable and gave a location where we could meet in one hour.

Deputy Pierce had taken photographs of the salt blocks along with a written statement from the big man while I had been dealing with his father. We had enough evidence and could file citations later. For now, we needed to hike back down the mountain and be on our way.

I snapped my portable radio back on my belt. We were a long way from Cemetery road. The whitetail was now state property, but the thought of dragging its bulky carcass for over a mile didn't appeal to me one bit. I cocked my head at the leviathan. "You killed it; you're going to take it back to my vehicle."

The giant stared at me quizzically for a moment. Then a broad and knowing smile filled his immense face. He nodded obligingly, bobbing his head in short, woodpecker strokes. Then he swept the drag-rope into his huge fist and we started back down the mountain. The poachers followed us, father shadowed by his lumbering son, who dragged the deer behind him as if it were no more than a rag doll.

Halfway down the mountain Dominic split off to join his father and resume hunting for the day. I thanked him for assisting us and continued downhill until I reached my patrol car. Once there, I loaded the confiscated deer onto my big game rack and informed the poachers that their citations would soon be forthcoming. Because they were non-residents, I could have hauled them before a judge to post bail. But time was passing fast, and we had to reach Jay. It was a judgment call that paid off, for later that month both men pled guilty and paid their fines in full.

Jay was waiting for us in a vacant parking lot at the edge of a broad meadow that led into a distant woodlot. He was eager to get started. "I hope they haven't left already," he said anxiously. "It's noon, and they might want lunch."

We shook hands. "We got here as fast as we could."

"Well, we better get started." he said. Motioning us to follow, he marched off like a captain leading his men into battle. Pierce and I trailed dutifully behind.

"I was pushing deer for my father when I saw them," he told me as I struggled to keep pace. "Neither of these guys is wearing orange and there was a bunch of shelled corn scattered by the one of their treestands. When I saw them, I waved a hello like I didn't know anything. Didn't want them to think I was on to 'em,"

"Excellent," I puffed.

He acknowledged with a sly grin. "Then I hoofed it out of there so I could call you." Jay stopped suddenly and pointed to a vehicle parked several hundred yards away. "That's their truck up on the hill. Guess they're still here after all."

We continued across the sweeping meadow, walking continuously downhill until we came to a large wooded area and began heading toward it. Suddenly Jay hit my shoulder with a firm backhand and we stopped dead. "Look! Somebody's down there."

A bearded man sporting an orange hat and vest was walking parallel to us through the trees a hundred yards ahead. We moved toward him fast. "State officer!" I called. "Stop where you are!"

He turned, saw us coming and waited.

He wasn't carrying a rifle, so I frisked him for concealed weapons but found nothing. I asked for identification. As I inspected his hunting license, Jay slipped behind him and faced me. Once again we had someone from New Jersey.

"Where is your gun?" I said.

"It's back at the truck with my brother. We were just leaving to get lunch when I realized I'd forgotten my tarsal gland. It's hanging by my treestand up ahead."

"Is that where you were hunting earlier?"

"Yeah."

I glanced at Jay. A leering smile of condemnation crossed his face as he slowly shook his head.

I nodded and leveled my gaze at the bearded man. "Are you sure about that?" I said.

He read my face and winced, realizing suddenly that the person standing behind him was the man he'd seen earlier that day—the same man who had walked so nonchalantly by him as he hunted from a baited treestand. It was over. There was no sense trying to lie his way out of anything.

He dropped his head in submission. "You got me," he breathed. "I was hunting further back in the woods—and yes, my stand has corn sprinkled about. The treestand up ahead is my brother's. Come on, I'll show you."

We walked another fifty feet to the first treestand and found no illegal bait. Then we followed our suspect another hundred yards into the woods before we came to a treestand with several bushels of cracked corn spread around it. After taking photographs of the bait, I grabbed a handful of corn and put it in a plastic sandwich bag. Then we proceeded out of the woods toward the pickup truck parked in a distant field. The poacher's brother sat stiffly inside the vehicle, watching as we approached. Two uniformed wardens and a witness escorting his brother was enough to convince him they'd been caught. After questioning him, he readily admitted to hunting deer in the same baited woodlot.

Over the years, I've had similar incidents where honest hunters willingly gave up their valuable time to assist in the apprehension and arrest of wildlife poachers. The eyes and ears of the public are a game warden's best friend. Please, get involved. Almost all wildlife agencies have a phone number dedicated as a poacher hotline. Game wardens, on average, are extremely dedicated enforcement officers. If you see a violation, take the time to call us. We will respond, and your efforts will be greatly appreciated.

Ambush at Dutch Mountain

AS THE FIRST GLINT of sun began to vaporize the early morning haze, he saw the bear coming toward him. It moved through the shadowed woodland in a heedless, plodding gait, savoring the breeze. The alluring scent of apples, corn, and lard promised a grand feast, as it had each day for many months. Winter was close at hand, food was all the bear needed or cared about. And it had become less wary in its haste.

Following a well-worn trail toward the bait, the bear never saw the poacher. Cradling a rifle with his back to a tree, he'd been waiting patiently for it to come within range. He'd traveled a long way in anticipation of this moment, clear across the state, in fact. A distance of almost three hundred miles.

It had been worth it. The abundant tracks and droppings at Tall Tree Camp indicated a number of large bears were working the bait. He shouldered his rifle and pointed it at the lumbering bruin. It would be the first one to go down today.

Cletus Clod steadied his aim as the bear padded toward him. It was close now. So close that he could see its dense coat shiver with every step it took.

And as the bear came broadside to him, he aimed behind its heavy shoulder and fired his first round . . . .

An anonymous tip brought me to Dutch Mountain later that same morning. The informant, a hunter out prospecting for bear sign, had discovered a number of baited hunting camps up on the plateau. Outraged by what he had found, he returned to his camp and called the Game Commission immediately.

My deputies were already spread out, checking other properties on the remote mountaintop, when Warden Larry Bundy and I arrived at Tall Tree Camp, a cozy wood-framed cabin nestled within a grove of lofty pines at the road's edge.

At first glance, everything appeared normal as I parked my patrol car in the tree-lined driveway. But as we started toward the back door to announce our presence, we froze in our tracks. Few times in our careers had Bundy or I ever seen such a flagrant case of unlawful baiting: Dozens of bread loaves had been scattered across the camp's manicured back yard, and a wooden utility pole by the cabin had been smeared with thick gobs of white grease as far as a man could reach. Bear claw marks sliced through the buttery coating in long grooves. Piles of yellow apples and grocery-fresh corncobs had been dumped here, too. Centered in the yard, a fifty-five-gallon steel barrel lay horizontally across a tree stump. It had been nailed down, the interior smeared with grease and then doused with a generous sprinkling of sunflower seeds. Adjacent to it, a fifty-pound salt block stood fresh and glistening white. Everything was in plain view of a large picture window at the rear of the cabin, so there was no question that anyone staying there would have to know the place was baited.

A well-worn bear trail entered the yard from the woods surrounding the property. Tracks and droppings indicated that a number of bears had become regular visitors. Some of their dung contained so much corn that it had turned yellow, taking on the appearance of a thick commercial cornmeal. Other droppings were heavily freckled with undigested apples and sunflower seeds. It was obvious that the bears had been feeding here for a long time. Years perhaps.

Bundy and I were about to follow the trail back into the woods when a man stepped unexpectedly from the cabin door. He wore a camouflage coat with matching trousers, his head covered by an orange hat. A big man, his face was broad and jowly and covered with stubble.

As we walked toward him he watched us with cautious eyes that seemed too narrow and too small for a man his size.

"State game warden," I said. "Your name, sir?"

"Name's Clod," he answered. "Cletus Clod."

"Been hunting today?"

"Shot a bear this morning. Just came back for my truck so I could haul it out of the woods."

"Where did you shoot it?"

Clod turned and pointed a stout finger behind him. "Back yonder. Maybe a quarter mile."

I nodded my head toward the bait. "How about all the food lying around back there, who did that?"

Barrel with sunflower seeds and white grease.

Clod looked over my shoulder into the yard and frowned. "I don't know nothing about that stuff," he said. "Never noticed it before."

"You never noticed it before?" I said in amazement. "How long have you been here?"

Clod's forehead bunched into thick wrinkles, like ham slices, his tiny eyes searching the blue sky while he mentally counted. "Ummm . . . three days. Been here since Friday."

"And in all that time you never noticed any of the bait that was here? How about the barrel on its side—didn't it seem unusual, lying on a tree stump like that?"

No response.

"Did you ever walk by that barrel?" I said. "Peek inside?

Clod began to rock on the balls of his feet, eyes shifting to the barrel and then back to me as he spoke. "Okay. I did look. But only once."

White grease pasted on telephone pole.

"How about the telephone pole, didn't you wonder about all that white stuff pasted on it like icing on a cake?"

He looked over at the pole and paused for a moment. Then he nodded in a kind of weary submission. "I guess I knew what it was. But I don't know how it got there."

"So, if you saw the barrel and the pole, you must have seen the bread loaves and the corn and the apples too. You must have known the camp was baited . . . right?"

Cletus Clod turned both hands toward me, his thick fingers splayed in a gesture of resignation. "Okay, okay. I admit I saw it . . . but I didn't put it there!"

The fact that he didn't supply the bait didn't get him off the hook. His knowledge of it was enough. He'd already admitted killing a bear, and I suspected it was close enough to the cabin to charge him with unlawful hunting. But I needed to find the carcass in order to cement my case. I asked to see the bear, hoping he would cooperate.

"Follow me," he said. "I'll show you where I shot it."

Clod climbed into his pickup truck and started down the township road while Bundy and I tailed him in my patrol car. He traveled a short distance before doing a one-eighty onto Dusty Road, a dirt lane that ran back toward Tall Tree Camp. A quarter-mile-wide neck of woods separated us from the bait when he parked his truck and got out.

"It's back in there," he pointed. "Maybe a hundred yards or so."

We followed as he led us through the wooded peninsula and soon came upon four men rolling a dolly through the trees with a large bear strapped to it.

"Right there's my bear," declared Clod. I immediately noticed that the bear wasn't gutted, and wondered if it was because they didn't want to leave the entrails behind to indicate where it had been killed.

The men stopped cold when they saw us. Game wardens are never a welcomed sight when you're breaking the law, and they never expected to see Cletus Clod leading two uniformed officers right to them. I ordered the men to stand where they were. They stared back at us with guilty faces.

One of them, a grayish man in his late sixties, looked straight at Clod. "What's this all about, Cletus?"

I cut in. "How many of you are hunting out of Tall Tree Camp?"

The hunters searched each others faces for a moment. Then the gray man spoke for them: "They're all with me," he said. "My camp lies up the road a quarter mile from here. We heard the shot and came over to investigate. Found Cletus with his bear, so we wanted to help him get it to the road. That's how things work around here, warden. We're all neighbors. Somebody needs something, we all pitch in."

"Tall Tree Camp is baited," I said. "I want you to understand something: this area is closed to hunting for the remainder of the season—"

"You can't be serious!" they cried.

"Oh, I'm serious all right. My deputies will be up here posting the plateau later today. You're going to have to find someplace else to hunt."

Then, while Bundy collected names and address from the hunting licenses of each man, I had Clod show me exactly where he killed the bear.

He led me deeper into the woods until we came to a tree stump where he'd been sitting. I saw five ejected bullet casings lying on the ground. Clod admitted they were his. I picked them up, dumped them in my pocket, and followed him another fifty feet through the brush. Here he pointed to a dried pool of blood. "This is where it fell," he said. "Took five shots to bring him down."

I looked into the woods toward Tall Tree Camp and saw a pathway coming toward us through the brush. It was a well-established bear trail that had likely been used for years.

"I'm taking your bear for evidence," I said.

"Evidence of what?"

"Hunting with bait."

He swiveled his head left and right. "But there ain't no bait out here! Do you see any bait?"

"Lots of it, and so did you, back at Tall Tree Camp."

"But I was nowhere near there when I shot my bear."

"You were hunting along a bear trail leading to the camp," I said flatly. "You'll be receiving citations for unlawful hunting. You can pay the fine or take a hearing. It's up to you."

Clod's face fell into a deep frown. "But I don't think I did anything wrong. If I take a hearing and win, will I get my bear back?"

"It'll be stored in a large evidence freezer," I told him. "If you're found not guilty, the bear is yours. Now, let's get it out of the woods."

We walked back to Clod's hunting buddies, and after enlisting their aid, began to haul the bear through the woods toward my patrol vehicle. Dragging a dolly loaded with a three hundred pound bear carcass across the broken, wooded terrain was a grueling chore. So, when we spotted an opening in the woods by a neighboring camp, we headed in that direction. As we transported the bear across the property, I noticed a lone apple lying in the lawn and made a mental note to return later for a closer look.

After wrestling with the bruin for another fifty yards, we finally reached my vehicle and rolled the shaggy beast off the dolly and onto my big game carrier. I released everyone after advising them that I had yet to determine if they would be prosecuted along with Cletus Clod for poaching. The men walked off shaking their heads and grumbling bitterly.

In truth, however, I doubted I could make a case against them. The hunters had come from a neighboring property, not Tall Tree Camp. Although I suspected they knew about the bait, I thought it unlikely that I'd ever be able to prove it.

Bundy and I returned to the woods with my three-hundred-foot tapeline, and, starting at the stump where I found Clod's empty shell casings, we began to take measurements back to Tall Tree Camp. Along the way, we found numerous piles of bear dung containing undigested corn, sunflower seeds, and apple chunks—the same type of food we discovered at the camp. When we broke through the woods and reached the baited fifty-five gallon drum, we had measured a distance of eight hundred feet.

After photographing everything at the camp, I took samples from both the telephone pole and the fifty-five gallon drum for evidence. Satisfied I had enough to successfully prosecute Cletus Clod, I started back to my vehicle with Officer Bundy.

When we reached my Chevy Blazer, Bundy went off to assist my deputies as they scoured the woods for additional violations while I grabbed a heavy rope and began to lash Clod's bear to my game carrier.

As I struggled with the carcass, I noticed a man watching me from the front porch of his cabin, thirty yards away. He was sitting in a wicker chair in the freezing cold, and when he saw me looking, he pushed himself up and ambled over.

"Need some help?" he asked casually.

"Wouldn't mind," I said. "What's your name, sir?"

"Tommy," he said. "Tommy Jynx." Tall and lanky, he had graying hair and a narrow, weathered face. After helping me maneuver the heavy carcass so I could tie it down, he stepped back and stared at me in a strange sort of way: like a condemned man awaiting his stroll to the gallows.

I finished securing the carcass, and for no other reason than to make small talk said, "See any bears besides this one today?"

He nodded. "Yup."

I waited for more words but they never came. He just stood there examining me with his gaze.

"Shoot any?" I asked, half joking.

"Yup," Jynx answered again, this time motioning toward his cabin, named Birch Camp. "It's in the back of my truck."

The apple . . . !

It came back to me in a flash! I'd seen it behind his cabin less than an hour ago; how could I have forgotten?

"Where did you shoot your bear?" I asked, knowing the answer even before he spoke.

"By my cabin," he said. "Stepped outside this morning and it was coming right at me, so I shot it."

I walked over to his pickup truck parked in the driveway and peered into the bed. A one hundred and fifty pound sow lay dead. It was properly tagged, but like Clod's bear, was not gutted. "Mind showing me where the bear stood when you pulled the trigger?"

Jynx motioned me to follow and we walked over to a lone apple tree in the middle of his back yard, the only tree on the half-acre lot. Two dozen apples were spread upon the grass by the trunk. But these were robust nursery apples, not the dwarfish, tortured kind that grow wild on Dutch Mountain. I dropped to one knee for a closer look and saw several drops of blood in the grass.

Standing, I turned toward Mr. Jynx. His cabin was directly behind him now, a window propped open on the second floor. I was certain that the bear had been ambushed from there. "These apples look like they came from a grocery store," I remarked. "And there is a big opening in the branches above us. They didn't fall from this tree. Someone put them here."

Tommy Jynx scratched his head absently. "Not me."

"But even so," I countered, "you can see the apples from your camp; you had to know they were here."

Suddenly my handheld radio came alive. It was Bundy. "Bill," he said. "Turn around and look across the road."

I pivoted and saw him waving at me from the back yard of a neighboring camp. I keyed the mike. "Find something?"

"There's more than a ton of corn piled behind this camp. Bear droppings all over the place, too."

"Ten-four, Larry," I said. "Get some photographs and samples for me."

"Working on it right now. Just wanted to let you know."

I turned to Tommy Jynx. "Let's take a walk."

We started toward the woods hemming his property and soon came across fresh bear dung in his yard. It was loaded with pieces of apple. I stopped and turned to him. "Look, Mr. Jynx, your property is centered between Tall Tree Camp and several others that have been heavily baited. I think you know what's going on around here. The apples under your tree didn't grow naturally and fall to the ground. Someone put them there. And I think that someone was you. I'm convinced that your bear was killed unlawfully, so I'm going to seize it and cite you for poaching."

Tommy Jynx, a man of few words, didn't utter a sound. He simply walked over to his truck, opened the tailgate, and began dragging his bear to my Blazer. I trailed close behind, and when we reached my vehicle, I helped him wrestle the bulky carcass onto the big game carrier. He stood there for a moment, gazing at his bear. Then he turned abruptly and walked to his cabin, closing the front door behind him.

I didn't know if he intended to take a hearing or not. And I don't think he knew himself at the time. I walked back to the scraggly apple tree and photographed the blood spatters on the grass and the apples that had been placed underneath it. I plucked a sample of the bloodied grass and took an apple from the ground for evidence. Then I snapped a photo of the open upstairs window at his cabin and returned to my vehicle to finish tying down his bear.

Later that day, I performed autopsies on both bears. The bullet path on Jynx's bear showed it had been killed from a well-placed large caliber projectile fired from an angle high above ground level. The slug had entered through the bear's upper shoulder in a downward angle, penetrating its heart and exiting near the bear's sternum. The trajectory left no doubt that it had been shot from the second story window of Jynx's cabin. I cut open the stomach and found it packed with undigested apples. As suspected, it had been gorging on them when it was killed. After carefully photographing the stomach contents, I moved my attention to Clod's bear. His animal had been hit with three out of the five shots he'd fired: once through the heart, and once through the lungs, with the third slug entering the bear's abdominal cavity. I cut open its stomach and found it packed with undigested yellow apples, corn kernels, sunflower seeds, and chunks of bread, leaving no doubt in my mind that it had been killed after feeding on the bait at Tall Tree Camp.

Later that week, I filed identical citations against Tommy Jynx and Cletus Clod. Both were charged with unlawfully killing a bear and hunting over bait. Tommy Jynx was quick to plead guilty by mail, and included a personal check to pay his one thousand dollar fine. But Cletus Clod decided to take his chances in court and hired the well-known and formidable attorney, David Posatko, to defend him. His trial before District Judge Patricia Robinson lasted a grueling eight hours, an unprecedented length of time for a non-jury summary trial. And when it finally ended, Clod was found guilty of both charges against him.

It was an important decision for me. Had Clod been found not guilty, the news would have traveled like wildfire, encouraging the practice of hunting with bait throughout the county. The courtroom had been packed with hunters who were convinced that Clod should have been found not guilty. They reasoned that if you couldn't see the bait from your hunting spot, then you were not "hunting over bait" per se.

Attorney Posatko agreed, arguing that the Game Law was unconstitutionally vague because it didn't specify what distance a hunter had to be from bait in order to be lawful. I had expected this argument and came prepared with a decision from the United States Court of Appeals where the court refused to define the limits of a baited area by a specific distance that a hunter must maintain from the bait. In doing so, the court stated the following: *The extent of a 'baited area' is defined only by the capacity of bait placed anywhere within it to act as an effective lure for the particular hunter charged. An arbitrary spatial limitation would fail to protect those animals that are attracted within shooting range by bait in areas just outside any arbitrary limitation that may be set.* In its opinion, the trial court also quoted a Pennsylvania Superior Court opinion that expressed a consistent view, which stated, *It would have been impossible for the legislature to delineate a specific area within which baiting in general could be limited. Animal habits and geography in the myriad of possible situations represent variables that defy reduction to a legislative formula.*

When Judge Robinson took these high court decisions under consideration, coupled with the fact that Clod had admitted to Bundy and me that he was aware of the bait at Tall Tree Camp, she had little difficulty finding him guilty.

But Cletus Clod proved to be a determined fighter who wasn't about to give up. He immediately appealed his guilty verdict to the Wyoming County Court of Common Pleas.

I was in for another tough court battle. Clod would be represented by the same attorney—a tenacious and often brilliant rival I had faced many times before—so I decided to take additional measures, laying groundwork that would ensure that I had the strongest evidence possible in order to establish a second guilty verdict . . .

A full year passed before Cletus Clod's appeal hearing started. Because this would be a precedent-setting case for the county, I asked District Attorney George Skumanick to handle it for me. Skumanick was an experienced prosecutor and an avid bear hunter. He reviewed the case with me and took an immediate interest in it, especially when he learned of the two new witnesses that I had arranged to testify for the Commonwealth.

One was Paul Daube, a forensic serologist for the Pennsylvania State Police Crime Laboratory in Harrisburg. An expert in forensic sciences, he had examined the stomach contents from Clod's bear as well as the bait samples taken from Tall Tree Camp. Daube was a trusted and credible expert witness who had testified in court many times in the past. My other witness was Doctor Gary Alt, a world famous wildlife biologist with a PhD in wildlife management. Alt specialized in the study of Pennsylvania black bears and had published many articles about their behavior. Although recognized chiefly for his vast experience with bears, he had given more than a thousand lectures on other wildlife management topics around the country throughout his career.

But before these two distinguished experts would take the stand, Skumanick needed to establish our case, bring the judge up to date on what had happened. He called me as his first witness, and, after being duly sworn in, he asked a series of questions that allowed me to illustrate what had taken place during my investigation.

Through Skumanick's questioning I was able to testify in detail about the bait at Tall Tree Camp and explain how Clod had killed his bear eight hundred feet away on a trail leading to it. As I testified, Skumanick introduced many of the photographs I had taken into evidence, virtually painting a picture of the day's events for the judge.

When I finished, Attorney Posatko had an opportunity to cross-examine me. The evidence presented against his client was convincing. Posatko knew it would be. After all, we'd gone through it all before at the district justice hearing with Judge Robinson.

And like any good defense attorney, he would put *me* on trial now. With an accusatory tone, he would grill me on everything I did—or failed to do—in the course of my investigation. If he could impair my credibility, make me backtrack on some testimony, show the court I'd erred in some procedural way, he might damage my case enough to get his client off. But in the end, his cross-examination, proved fruitless. The evidence against his client was simply too strong.

Skumanick called forensics expert Paul Daube next. Daube testified about the evidence I had brought to the Crime Lab almost a year earlier. They were two separate packages: one marked STOMACH CONTENTS containing a sample of food items extracted from the stomach of Clod's bear, the other marked SUSPECTED BAIT, which contained grease extracted from the barrel and the utility pole at Tall Tree Camp along with some kernels of corn.

Daube told the court that the contents from both packages were placed in an infrared spectrophotometer for comparison purposes. This instrument emits a heat beam that gives a "fingerprint" of compounds via infrared energy, he explained, thereby providing valuable information about the structure of the compounds—in this case, corn and grease.

Mr. Daube further testified that in his expert opinion the forensic examination revealed that the corn and grease taken from the barrel and the utility pole at Tall Tree Camp were related in both appearance and nature to the samples taken from the bear's stomach. They were, in essence, the same.

The defense attorney tried to muddle Daube's findings as best he could, but the scientist's testimony had provided inarguable evidence that Clod's bear had been feeding on the bait at Tall Tree Camp prior to being killed.

Skumanick's next witness was Officer Larry Bundy. His testimony mirrored my earlier statements about the case, adding credence to everything I had testified to. In his cross-examination, Attorney Posatko took particular exception to

Bundy's testimony that Cletus Clod admitted being aware of the bait at Tall Tree Camp.

"Isn't it a fact," he said to Bundy, "that the only thing Mr. Clod told you was that he knew about a barrel and a utility pole in the yard as opposed to knowing some type of grease was on it?"

"That's not true," countered Bundy. "He was aware of the grease. His exact words were, 'I knew it was there, but I didn't put it there.'"

Attorney Posatko was painfully aware that his client's knowledge of the bait at Tall Tree Camp would hamper his defense. But the worst was yet to come for the attorney when Skumanick called his final witness.

Doctor Gary Alt stepped up to Judge Vanston's massive wooden desk and sat in the witness chair to his left. Alt, in his mid-forties, was dressed in a neatly pressed white shirt with a blue tie and khaki pants. He adjusted his seat and looked directly at the district attorney, his gaze exuding a composed self-confidence.

"Dr. Alt, could you tell the court how you're employed?" asked the District Attorney (DA).

Alt: "I'm a wildlife research biologist for the Pennsylvania Game Commission."

DA: "And could you tell the court your educational background?"

Alt: "I have an Associate Degree, a B.S., an M.S., and a Ph.D. in Wildlife Management."

DA: "And how long have you been dealing in Wildlife Management?"

Alt: "I've been studying bears for twenty-one years."

DA: "Do you specialize in any one type of bear?"

Alt: "Black bears here in Pennsylvania."

DA: "And have you ever been certified as an expert in any court of law on the topic of black bears?"

Alt: "On many occasions."

DA: (addressing the judge) "We would simply ask that Dr. Alt be certified as an expert in black bears and Wildlife Biology."

Judge Vanston: "Mr. Posatko, do you wish to examine Dr. Alt?"

Posatko: "No, Your Honor, I do not."

Judge Vanston: "The court accepts Dr. Alt in the stated categories as an expert. Go ahead, Mr. Skumanick."

DA: "Doctor, could you tell the court, what are the characteristic habits of black bears in late November?"

Alt: "At that time of year, bears are in what we call a hyperphagic stage, and what that means is that they're gorging themselves to gain weight to prepare for hibernation; and in fact, studies have indicated they're eating typically in excess of twenty thousand calories a day."

DA: "And what type of food stuffs would a bear go after to get those sorts of calories?"

Alt: "Well, in all three species of bears, certainly in black bears here, the simplest way I can describe this is calories per hour. They're going for the highest number of calories that they can get."

DA: "And could you tell the court, would a black bear be attracted to grease if it was available?"

Alt: "Yes, grease is a powerful attractant for bears."

DA: "And if grease is put out for a bear, will a bear continuously return to that area to seek out that grease?"

Alt: "Once the pattern has been established and the need for nutrition continues, they will often repeatedly come back and look for this food if they've had past experience of getting it someplace."

Skumanick then showed Dr. Alt photographs of the telephone pole smeared with grease at Tall Tree Camp. "Do you see any markings on those photos that you would consider significant?" he asked.

Alt: "Yes, this is being used by bears. It's what we call a marker tree or marking station. Of course, this is not a tree. This is a telephone pole but the bears are using it. What that means is that we [humans] communicate verbally, and our world is painted in vision and in vocalizations. In the world of the bear, many of these communications are done through the sense of smell, and they rub their bodies and leave visual cues on these marker trees. That's how they communicate who's in the area."

DA: "So if a bear, for example, were to mark that pole as part of his area, if subsequently someone were to put grease on that pole, would that draw the bear back to that same pole again?"

Alt: "If I were trying to put out a food item that I wanted a bear to find I would put it at a marker tree because this is where the bears go to check to see who else is there. It's not a matter of defending their territory per se. It's a matter of advertising their presence. And so, bears will nearly always investigate these marker trees. They'll smell it, rub on it, and move on. The next one comes along and does the same thing. It's very common. This is what you'd expect a bear to do."

DA: "Assuming the substance on the pole is grease, how far away could a bear smell that substance?"

Alt: "We know that dogs and polar bears can smell seals under three feet of snow for greater than one-half mile. That's been shown repeatedly. And I am certain that black bears have a tremendous sense of smell. We've seen them locking on food sources distantly. I haven't measured the distance but I would, in my opinion, assume they could smell the grease for a distance of at least one-half mile downwind."

DA: "What is the typical range, during the day, of a black bear?"

Alt: "The home range for females is three to five miles in diameter. Males, ten to fifteen miles. But in late fall their home ranges shrink down. It's a seasonal thing. They lock in on food sources and may spend over ninety percent of their time in an area of one square mile during late November."

DA: "You were in the courtroom when Officer Wasserman testified about the food sources found at various camps and the distances, would it be unusual for a bear to travel those distances to another food source?"

Alt: "No, this is classic. I have personally captured over three thousand bears, and hundreds and hundreds of them were caught in a scenario very similar to what I heard this morning, where they go from one camp to another. That's the way they feed . . . that's how we capture them. They go from one concentration of food resources to the next. The other thing, which is very common, is that they go from those concentrated food resources to denser cover where they'll bed. When they get hungry they return to the food resources, establishing regular trails between these food sources and the bedding areas."

DA: "Would bears be attracted to grease, bread, apples, and sunflower seeds?"

Alt: "Yes, it's common knowledge that they will knock down bird feeders especially for sunflower seeds. I just came back from Minnesota two weeks ago, and we tested a variety of foods on black bears. Grease is one of the items that they will fight for. They will literally fight over getting at that grease barrel even though there are lots of other types of food. Grease is a very powerful attractant. The most dominant, most powerful bears will monopolize the grease barrel while less dominant bears might be relegated to go over and feed on something else."

DA: "Would the bear repeatedly return to those areas?"

Alt: "When they run out of natural food they come as far as a hundred miles away to these feeding stations. Once they learn that there's food there every fall, large numbers of bears will come from a very large area and feed there until they're sufficiently obese that they can survive the winter."

DA: "So the testimony, maps, drawings, and photographs shown in court today depicting the trail leading from Tall Tree Camp to Birch Camp would be typical of bears?"

Alt: "Well, it's very typical of bears in an area of high food concentrations because bears, like many wild animals, are kind of lazy and they'll take the path of least resistance. So once a trail is established, they'll dependently walk it over and over and over."

DA: "Nothing further Your Honor . . ."

When Judge Vanston called on Attorney Posatko for cross-examination, he put forth a valiant effort, but there was little he could do to counter the doctor's eye-opening testimony. Posatko asked Alt to take a second look at the photographs of the fifty-five gallon drum and the utility pole, attempting to get him to back off some of his statements. But Dr. Alt remained steadfast in his testimony, and after being grilled for more than thirty minutes he was finally excused from the witness stand.

District Attorney Skumanick had nothing more to offer. All his witnesses had been called, and the Commonwealth rested its case.

It was time for the defense attorney to call witnesses in behalf of Cletus Clod. He called only one: Mr. Clod himself, who testified that he never noticed any of the bait at the camp—although he admitted having arrived there three days prior to the opening day of bear season—until Bundy and I pointed it out to him. He just happened to be posted in the woods when a bear came by, he claimed, maintaining that he had no idea he was standing along an active bear trail leading back to Tall Tree Camp when he shot his bear.

When Cletus Clod finished telling his side of the story, the district attorney approached the witness stand with a photograph in his hand. "Does this photograph depict the barrel, the stump, and telephone pole at Tall Tree Camp?"

"Yes, sir," answered Clod.

DA: "Did you tell Officer Wasserman in the presence of Officer Bundy that you knew the grease, the corn, and the sunflower seeds were there but that you didn't put the stuff there?"

Clod: "No, sir."

DA: "Did you hear Officer Wasserman and Officer Bundy testify earlier?"

Clod: "Yes, sir."

DA: "So, you're saying they're wrong?"

Clod: "Apparently they're mistaken."

DA: "Didn't it strike you as odd that somebody would place a barrel horizontally on the stump that way?"

Clod: "Maybe the man had a reason for it. It's not my cabin. Maybe he fed the animals."

DA: "You testified that you didn't walk by that barrel or telephone pole or anything during the three days you were there and that you never saw any of the grease, the corn, the sunflower seeds, or anything that was laying there?"

Clod: "No, I didn't go over there at all."

DA: (handing him a photograph) "Would you agree that this is a telephone pole?"

Clod: "It looks like a pole."

DA: "Would you agree with me that the photo also depicts a white substance smeared up and down the pole?"

Clod: "Yes, sir."

DA: "Can you see the pole from the windows of the camp and from the porch?"

Clod: "Yes, sir."

DA: "But you didn't see any of the white substance on the pole?"

Clod: "I didn't notice it looking like that. Maybe it looks different with the eye than it does with a camera."

DA: "Well, wouldn't you agree with me that the pole depicted was taken from a distance away, that it's not a close up photograph?"

Clod: "Yes, sir."

DA: "And you can clearly see a white substance, grease, smeared up and down the pole?"

Clod: "I see something. But I don't know what it is."

DA: (handing Clod another photograph) "You're saying the bear wasn't coming down this trail as testified to by Wasserman earlier?"

Clod: "I didn't see no trail."

DA: "You didn't see a trail . . . ? Take another look at the photograph. Wouldn't you agree that there appears to be a worn area in the grass and through the brush and shrubs?"

Clod: (becoming increasingly nervous and frustrated) "Wherever that's at—it's something. I don't know where that's at though."

DA: (leaning toward the defendant) "Well, did you hear Officer Wasserman testify earlier that this was the same trail where you shot the bear and that it was leading directly into Tall Tree Camp?"

Clod: "I heard him say that."

DA: "Would you agree with me that there is a large area of land you can hunt up there (referring to over a hundred thousand acres of State Game Lands bordering Tall Tree Camp)?"

Clod: "Oh, yes, sir."

DA: "And yet you chose to hunt eight hundred feet away from the cabin?"

Clod: "Because we seen bear sign over there."

DA: "It wouldn't be because you knew that there was bait at your cabin and bait at Birch Camp?"

Clod: "No, sir."

DA: "Nothing further Your Honor . . ."

The trial had dragged on for most of the day. A considerable amount of testimony had been heard, and I fully expected the judge to adjourn the court and reserve his decision for a later date, as judges often do when they've presided over a lengthy case. But to my surprise, Judge Vanston rendered his decision immediately.

"The evidence is closed," he said. "It is clear to me that Tall Tree Camp and several other camps in the area were illegally baited. No question about that. The next question is did the defendant have knowledge of the baiting and use it in furtherance of his hunting or attempted hunting?

"The court finds the defendant's testimony absolutely incredible. The court believes that any reasonable, experienced hunter would have had an affirmative obligation upon looking out the porch or the window or the back door of this camp, and seeing what is obvious from the photographs, to investigate it to determine if it's bait. The verdict of the court on each count is guilty."

Cletus Clod was sentenced to pay the maximum fine at that time: one thousand dollars plus three years revocation of his hunting and trapping privileges in Pennsylvania. But Clod was determined to pursue the matter further and appealed his case to the Commonwealth Court of Pennsylvania. Months later, the higher court, which consisted of a three-judge panel in Harrisburg, upheld Clod's guilty verdict in Wyoming County.

I was grateful for both decisions. Prior to that year, 1994, there had been no high court opinions in Wyoming County regarding hunting through the use of bait. As a result, the three district justices responsible for the initial adjudication of most cases could have differing opinions (a sure bet, in fact) about what constituted unlawful hunting if some type of food had been placed in the immediate area to attract game.

Now we had written opinions from both the President Judge of Wyoming County and the Commonwealth Court of Pennsylvania, stating, essentially, that if a hunter is aware of bait, even if he is hunting eight hundred feet away, he is hunting unlawfully.

The Clod case was one of three important bait cases in my career. There were two more that followed. Each involved incidents where the hunter was considerably farther from the bait than Cletus Clod when they were arrested. One case went all the way to the Pennsylvania Supreme Court after being appealed three separate times over a five-year period. It was the most important case of my career. You can read about it in my companion book *Game Warden: Adventures of a Wildlife Warrior.*

Bonnie and Clyde

JUST OVER A YEAR had passed since I'd first met Clyde. Broad shouldered and squat, he was halfway through a tuna sandwich when he came to the door, his lunch sticking to his throat when he saw me. He stepped outside, swallowed hard, and sputtered, "Help ya?"

"Yes, Clyde, you can," I assured him. "I want to talk to you about the deer you shot last night."

Clyde studied his sandwich for a moment, then he puckered his lips and squinted. "Deer?"

"Now, Clyde," I cautioned, "before you say anything else, I want you to know I have an eyewitness who saw everything."

Clyde frowned at the notion that he'd been ratted on, his face turning scarlet.

I pressed him for an answer. "The man is your neighbor. He says you shot the deer in his front lawn and parked your truck in his driveway to go look for it. You must've known he'd call."

"But I needed the meat," Clyde groaned. "Jobs have been few and far between, lately." He paused for a long moment, then shook his head with regret. "No sense lying about it— you got me. What comes next, a big fine?"

I ignored the question. "What time was it when you shot the deer?"

"I don't know—after ten for sure. I was across the road on my buddy's front porch when we saw it standing there in the moonlight, all big and dumb like. So I shot it. Never found the carcass. Didn't spend much time looking either, since, like you said, I was parked right in my neighbor's driveway. Saw his lights go on. Figured he'd call. Guess I'm not surprised you're here."

"Is there someplace we can sit down?" I asked. "I have some writing to do."

Clyde glanced at his sandwich then back at me. "Come on in; I was just having lunch." He turned, and I trailed him into the kitchen.

We took seats at the table and I pulled some papers from my coat pocket. Clyde set his sandwich down, scratched absently at the day-old stubble on his chin, and leaned back on his chair. "You gonna write me a ticket?"

"Yes, Clyde," I said. "But first I'd like you to write down exactly what happened. I have the necessary paperwork with me. Mind?"

"Nope! Hand them documents over; I'll tell you exactly what happened. Only . . ."

He paused, lips pressed into a thin white line.

"Only what, Clyde?"

"Somebody was with me when I went for the deer. I don't want them to get into trouble for what I did. I mean, we never even found the danged thing. *I* shot it! I'll admit to it. But this should be between you and me and nobody else."

"Fair enough." I said.

Clyde straightened in his chair and peered at me skeptically. "You mean, you don't care?"

"Oh, I care all right. But that's not the point. You've been honest with me, Clyde. You've answered all my questions, and you admit killing the deer. One deer, one man, one fine. That seems fair enough to me. Tell your friend he got off lucky this time."

I slid a pen and paper across the table. Clyde set it in front of him and paused to study my face. Then, nodding in just agreement, he reached for the pen and began to write his confession . . .

And now, fourteen months later, I found myself paying another visit to the man. I had received a phone call, the voice telling me that Clyde had killed a buck and had it hanging from a tree by his house. It was eleven p.m. when

Deputy Pierce and I pulled into his driveway and stopped to look around.

"What's the fine going to be this time?" asked Pierce.

"At least six hundred," I said as I unbuckled my seat belt. "His license was revoked for the deer he shot last year, so if he killed another one it can't be legal. I guess some people never learn."

"Guess not," agreed Pierce.

"Thing is, I don't see a deer hanging from a tree anywhere, do you?"

Pierce raised his binoculars and scanned the property. "Nope!" he said. "Don't see a thing."

"Then we're pulling out. It's late, and I don't have a search warrant. Besides, Clyde may not be home. His truck isn't here."

The following morning, I called my informant to double check on the story he'd given me and learned we had been at the wrong house. Although I had arrested Clyde there last year and assumed it was his home, it was in fact, his mother's. Clyde's place, I was told, could be found by following the private dirt lane another hundred yards into the woods. His house was at the end of the drive, my informant assured me. And the deer was still there, hanging from a tree.

I hung up and made a call to my neighboring officer, Joe Wenzel, asking if he could assist with the case. Joe and I had worked together many times through the years, and he was a good friend. I was pleased when he said he could come.

The sky was overcast and gray with a light snow-cover on the ground as we inched along the narrow lane approaching Clyde's house. Rounding a final bend in the road, Wenzel suddenly pointed out the windshield. "There's a buck hanging from a tree to our left. This must be the place."

"Isolated," I said. "Never would have found it if someone hadn't told me the house was here."

I stopped by a small sedan parked behind Clyde's house and killed the ignition. "Looks like somebody's home."

We walked to the doorway and knocked. Soon a woman appeared. She was in her mid-twenties, blonde, blue-eyed, slim. "Morning, ma'am," I said. "We're with the Pennsylvania Game Commission. Is Clyde home?"

The woman looked us over suspiciously. "Clyde's at work, and I don't expect him back until this evening. Is there a problem?"

Wenzel turned and started toward the buck, a six-pointer. "We have information that Clyde killed a deer." I said. "Is that his buck?"

"Oh, no, no, no. I shot that deer yesterday." She hesitated as Wenzel reached the carcass. Her eyes wide and pleading, she quickly added, "But I couldn't find my hunting license, so Clyde took a tag from one of his old licenses and put it on the deer."

I called out for Joe to pull the tag. He detached it from the buck's ear and walked back and handed it to me. "It's Clyde's tag all right," he said, shaking his head critically.

It was dated for the current year, making it illegal since Clyde's hunting privileges were revoked.

I dropped it in my coat pocket. "Excuse me, ma'am, but I thought you said the tag came from an *old* license?"

Her face dropped into an ugly scowl. "What difference does it make? It's tagged, isn't it!"

"It makes a difference to *me*," I assured her. "I want to see your hunting license and some identification."

The woman wheeled and stormed into her house. Returning seconds later with a hunting license in her hand, she thrust it toward me. I took the license and examined it. "Where were you when you shot the deer?"

She pointed past me. "Over there, in the brush."

"Where did you hit it?"

"In the chest."

"Right side or left?"

Her body stiffened. "I don't know!" she said angrily. "All I could see was the horns. The brush was too thick!"

Wenzel cut in. "Ma'am, I just examined your deer. It was shot in the neck. There are no chest wounds."

She put her hands on her hips and glared at us. "I'm starting to get sick and tired of all your questions. I want you off my property, right now!"

"It doesn't work that way, ma'am," I said. "And you still haven't shown me any identification."

"What do you mean? I just gave you my hunting license, you jerk!"

"That's not identification, ma'am. I want to see a driver's license if you have one."

Her expression suddenly changed as if she'd just remembered something. Then, with an abrupt about-face, she marched back into her house and returned with a driver's license in one hand and a cell phone in the other. I took the license and examined it while she began thumbing buttons on her phone.

"This is an expired Nevada driver's license," I said. "You couldn't have been issued a Pennsylvania hunting license with this—"

She thrust her cell phone in my face and quickly snapped it back. "I have the state police on the phone right now!" she said triumphantly. "Hello, trooper? This is Bonnie Blather. There are two game wardens on my property, and I want them removed!"

I heard a brief, muffled response on her phone.

"Excuse me!" she yelped. There came an expression of bewilderment: "Yes, one is Wasserman—but. Yes, but . . .! "

Her body wilted as she handed me the phone. "They want to talk to . . . *you!*"

I took it from her. "Wasserman," I answered.

"Bill, is everything under control? Do you need backup?"

"Everything is okay," I said. "We're working on a deer case and should be leaving shortly."

"Ten-four. Call if you need us."

I handed back the phone. "I still need to see some identification. Something that shows you're a Pennsylvania resident."

"What for?"

"So I can write you a citation for poaching."

She stood there, blinking stupidly.

"Your choice," I said. "You can cooperate and show me something or I can place you under arrest."

Once again, she stormed back into the house. I could hear her rummaging about, pulling dresser drawers and shuffling through papers. After several minutes she returned with a recent pay stub and handed it to me.

I looked it over. "The address on this receipt doesn't match the one on your hunting license."

"It's all I had when I bought the license. What else was I supposed to do?"

"Don't buy one—not until you can provide proper identification. Your license is illegal. I also don't believe you shot the deer, so I'm taking it. You and Clyde will have your citations mailed once I sort out the charges."

"Go ahead, take it you scum!" she shrieked. "Just get the hell off my property!"

And with those parting words of farewell, I loaded the illegal deer on my big game rack, and happily withdrew.

Later that week, I filed charges against Clyde for hunting while on revocation and for unlawfully killing a deer. Bonnie was charged with assisting in the unlawful killing of a deer, failure to take a hunter education course, and procuring a hunting license with an improper address.

Bonnie and Clyde elected to have a trial before a district judge. Bonnie testified under oath that she killed the deer, and Clyde backed her up. The judge didn't believe a word they said, and both were found guilty of all charges. Their fines and court costs totaled over fourteen-hundred dollars. In addition, Clyde had five years added to his already lengthy revocation period, while Bonnie had her hunting privileges revoked for three years.

Later that year I heard that Clyde found out which neighbor turned him in and challenged him to a fight. I'm told he was accommodated. As a result, Clyde's nose has acquired a peculiar new look these days.

Sinbad

THEY NEVER NOTICED him as they picked their way along the frozen hillside. He was crouched low behind a rotting stump, his ten-power scope zeroed in on the biggest of them. He watched for a moment, its head in the air and tilted slightly, as if, perhaps, it sensed its own impending doom.

Centering his crosshairs on the turkey's skull, he expelled a long breath through his nostrils and slowly squeezed the trigger. The rifle barked, its echo rolling through the valley like a low thunder. And as the turkey reeled across the snow covered meadow, the remaining flock began to scatter in a wild frenzy. But the poacher fired again, killing another before it could disappear into the surrounding woods.

He stood and filled his lungs with fresh air. The morning crisp and clear, and the snow so bright against the sun that his eyes hurt to look at it. This would be the beginning of another good season, he thought as he slung his rifle over a shoulder. Then he advanced toward his kill in great, jubilant strides.

It was early March, spring gobbler season more than six weeks away. But Sinbad didn't concern himself with seasons and bag limits. Nor did he care that he was on posted property. He regarded the law only with disdain. An outlaw and a bully, Sinbad took what he wanted in life. And woe to anyone who tried to stop him.

He retrieved his two birds and carried them to the ATV he'd hidden in the woods. Dropping the carcasses on the floorboards, he climbed aboard and keyed the ignition. He lived just over the mountain, and he intended to be long gone before anyone caught him here. But as he raced through the blazing white snow with his kill, the landowner had already begun to track him.

Michael Mills had heard the gunshots from inside his house. They had come from the hillside three hundred yards away. He quickly donned his coat and slipped into a pair of hiking shoes. Then he started marching across the snow until he came to a trail of heavy boot prints. Their depth told him the poacher weighed over two hundred pounds. His path easy to follow in the white powder, it soon showed where he'd retrieved two dead turkeys and then boarded his four-wheeler. And while Sinbad was on his way home to stash his kill, the landowner started to work his way toward him . . .

W hen State Game Warden Don Burchell was dispatched to investigate the incident, I happened to be patrolling close by and called him by radio to assist with the case. Although Sinbad lived in Burchell's patrol zone, his house was only a few hundred yards over the county line from my district. I met Burchell along a rural dirt road not far from Sinbad's trailer before we moved in on him.

"I want to give you a heads up about this guy," I said. "He comes from a long line of outlaws living in Wyoming County. I've arrested both of his brothers and most of his cousins over the years."

"What about this one?" said Burchell. "Ever run into him before?"

"No, but if he's anything like his brothers, we'll have our work cut out for us."

After parking our marked patrol cars in front of Sinbad's trailer, we went to the front door and banged on it. When no one answered we walked a short distance to a neighboring trailer. I knocked and the door cracked open. An elderly man eyed us suspiciously through the narrow space.

"Afternoon, sir," said Burchell.

The man said nothing; instead, he blinked with grim realization at our uniforms, then slowly closed the door.

The man's house was just to the left of Sinbad's. From where we stood, we could see the rear end of a red ATV poking from around the back corner.

"There's the four-wheeler," I said.

Burchell nodded. "He might be hiding in his trailer, watching us."

"I'll bet if we go over there and start snooping around we'll soon find out."

A faint smile crossed Burchell's face. "I was just thinking the same thing."

When we walked over to the ATV, we saw blood spatters on the rear fender. I nodded with satisfaction as Burchell stooped and picked a turkey's breast-feather from the floorboard. He pulled a small brown envelope from his coat pocket and dropped the feather inside.

Behind us, there was a large storage shed by the woods' edge, fifty yards away. A well-worn foot trail led directly to it through the snow. Burchell started toward the structure. I followed close behind.

The wood-planked eight-foot-square building displayed a large window by the front door. We peered into it and saw a workshop with tools hanging from the walls over a sturdy handmade bench. Lying on the bench were a pair of lopping shears and the severed feet of two wild turkeys.

"Souvenirs," remarked Burchell, shaking his head with disgust. "Let's head back to the trailer. We have enough to make an arrest; with any luck, he'll confess to everything. If not we can always get a search warrant."

As we turned to head back, Burchell suddenly veered toward a smoldering mound of charred brush.

"See something?" I asked.

"Not yet. But I have a hunch."

As we stood at the edge of the smoky heap, I followed Burchell's gaze.

"There! See it?" he said.

I refocused and spotted the blackened head of a turkey peeking from under a charred board. It had been badly burned. Burchell pulled a stout branch from the edge of the pile and shook off the burning embers. Then he began moving it through the heavy ashes like a sorcerer stirring a mystical kettle of stew. Soon the charred heads and wings of two adult gobblers rolled to the surface.

We got back to Sinbad's place just as a Chevy sedan pulled into the driveway. A women in her mid-twenties sat behind the wheel. She seemed genuinely surprised to see us.

She rolled down her window into the sun. "Can I help you?"

"We're with the State Game Commission," I said. "Do you live here?"

"Yes. Is something wrong, officer?"

"Do you have some identification with you, ma'am?"

"Of course I do, but I haven't been hunting!"

"Do you know Omar Sinbad?"

"Yes," she said, her face suddenly lined with concern. "I'm his wife." She exited her vehicle and opened her purse. "I have my driver's license in here somewhere," she said digging around for it. She offered it to Burchell with a trembling hand.

He took the license and wrote her name and address in a notepad. "Who owns the ATV around back?"

"My husband does. Now, could you please tell me what this is all about?"

"Omar killed two turkeys this morning," said Burchell. "We found blood and feathers on his ATV, and we believe the turkeys are in your house. We'd like to take a look."

She glanced at her trailer. "I . . . I don't know . . . my husband isn't here right now. He might not like the idea of me letting you inside. Can you wait till he comes back?"

"When do you expect him home?" said Burchell.

She looked at her watch. "Probably around five o'clock. He went to New Jersey for a job."

Burchell and I exchanged glances of disapproval. "Ma'am," I said. "That would be six hours from now. I don't think we can wait that long."

"Oh, this is terrible," she said nervously. "I don't know what to do!"

I sensed that her growing dismay was not for her own well-being but rather for her husband and what might happen to him if she let us in. It was an all too familiar scene: the husband's thoughtless and often reckless disregard for the law causing embarrassment and hardship for his family. I'd witnessed it many times. And although I felt empathy toward the woman, I still had a job to do. So, with a persuasive urging, I said, "Look, ma'am, we have plenty of evidence against your husband—enough to get a search warrant if we have to. I don't think you want that. Why don't you just bring the turkeys out to us? Get this whole thing over with. We're going to find them anyway, one way or another."

She stared at us, lips twitching in tiny spasms of frustration, eyes pleading, wishing, I suppose, that we'd simply disappear into thin air. "I'm really getting upset," she moaned desperately. "I'm going inside to call my father." She dropped her chin and turned away from us. Burchell and I stood helplessly by as she walked through the snow into her trailer and closed the door behind her.

Search warrants can be difficult to obtain, even under the best of circumstances. We hoped her father would persuade her to be more cooperative; otherwise, we'd have no choice but to head for town and see a district judge about the warrant, certain that the charred turkey parts recovered in the burn pile and the fresh blood on Sinbad's ATV would be enough to convince any judge to grant one.

It took only minutes before a pickup truck came cruising along the dirt road toward us and pulled into the driveway. A man in his late forties with salt-and-pepper hair stepped out and closed the door behind him. "Afternoon, officers," he said. "My daughter called and asked me to come over here. She sounded upset. What seems to be the problem?"

Burchell told him about the turkeys, explaining that we were prepared to obtain a search warrant but would prefer his daughter's cooperation instead.

He shook his head, lips pressed tightly. "Her husband has always been trouble," he muttered. "Let me talk to her for a minute. Maybe I can reason with her."

Once again, we found ourselves waiting. And it was getting tiresome. More than a half-hour passed, and when her father finally exited the trailer, he walked directly to his truck without so much as a glance in our direction. He jerked open the door and slid behind the wheel. Then he looked up at us and shook his head with regret before backing his vehicle from the driveway.

Sinbad's wife stepped out the front door, eyes red and puffy with tears. "You'll have to get a search warrant if you want to come in," she sobbed. "I have nothing more to say."

"I understand," Burchell said. There was an underlying tone of resignation in his voice knowing he'd have to head to town for the warrant. "Officer Wasserman is going to stay here. You'll have to remain on your property until I return."

The woman nodded back at him, then turned and closed the door behind her.

Though it took three long hours, Burchell had done his job well. The warrant he obtained authorized us to search Sinbad's trailer along with all outbuildings and vehicles on the property—and to seize any firearms, ammunition, wildlife, and other items we found pertaining to our investigation.

Before we started, I radioed our dispatcher, Barney Dobinick, explaining that we were about to search Sinbad's property and needed a pickup truck to haul his ATV for evidence. Barney happened to live on the opposite side of the mountain.

"I'll be off duty shortly," he said. "We can use my truck; see you in about thirty minutes."

Burchell and I began our search by collecting the severed turkey feet in Sinbad's workshop. Then we proceeded to the burn pile and bagged the charred body parts we'd discovered earlier. After securing everything in Burchell's vehicle, we moved to Sinbad's trailer and knocked. His wife came to the door, eyes puffy with tears. We handed her a copy of the warrant. She examined it, reading carefully, before stepping back out of our way.

"We'd like you to stay with us as we go through your house," Burchell told her.

She followed dutifully as we walked through her tiny living room into the kitchen. Burchell stepped over to the refrigerator and opened it. On the top shelf we saw an uncovered pot with a dressed wild turkey half submerged in water. Burchell took the pot to the kitchen sink and drained it. We placed the bird into a large plastic bag, then tied it closed and marked it with a yellow evidence tag.

"Where does your husband keep his guns?" I asked.

"In the back room," she said, her face a dark cloud of despair. "The one without a door."

We walked down a narrow hall to a doorway cloaked with a plastic shower curtain. I slid it aside and stepped into a room the size of a large walk-in closet. Reloading equipment, hunting gear, rifle scopes, and other supplies lay scattered about. A Winchester rifle leaned against the wall to my right. I put the muzzle to my nose; it smelled freshly fired. Certain I had the gun Sinbad used to kill the turkeys, I handed it to Burchell and started sorting through a low chest of drawers crammed with cartridge boxes. When I got to the bottom one, I saw a plastic sandwich bag filled with tiny dried leaves. My head whipped toward Burchell. "Marijuana!"

Sinbad's wife clutched at her stomach, "Oh, no!" She gasped. "It *can't* be! My husband would never use drugs!"

"It sure looks like marijuana to me," I said. "We'll find out for sure when we take it to the lab." I grabbed a handful of thirty-caliber bullets and the suspected weed and headed for the front door.

"Wait!" she pleaded. "You said you were looking for turkeys. You can't just come into my house and walk off with that stuff, can you?"

"Ma'am, I know what I have here: it's marijuana. Sorry, but I don't have a choice at this point."

There was only a little bit of weed, a small sandwich bag half filled. But I thought it might be an important bargaining chip if the case went to a court trial—a violation the district attorney might be willing to dismiss if Sinbad agreed to confess to charges of poaching.

I left the trailer and started toward my patrol car with the evidence when a beat-up pickup flew into the driveway and slammed to a screeching halt. The truck looked like it just came from a local demolition derby. The driver jumped out and strode toward me. "What the hell is going on here!"

I stopped along the walkway, my left side forward, knees bent slightly for balance, right leg poised for a kick to the groin or solar plexus. "Stop right there!" I commanded. I was in full uniform, badge on my chest, marked patrol car parked out front. There was no mistaking who I was.

He stopped just outside striking distance. Standing over six-feet tall, a red, lion's mane tumbled past yardstick-wide shoulders, his lips frozen into an ugly snarl. "You got no business being in my house!"

I reached inside my coat. "I have a warrant—"

"This is a bunch of crap!" he cried, cutting me off. Thick fingers curled into a hard fist, his face dark and menacing. A physical confrontation seemed imminent. And though I realized that at a time like this, the right words can be an officer's best defense, finding those words, especially in the heat of the moment, can be challenging at best.

In Sinbad's case, maybe impossible.

What could I say that would snap this two hundred and fifty pound enraged poacher to his senses? In a flash, it came to me: I pulled out the plastic bag. "Your wife isn't too happy about this."

He whipped his head toward the trailer, blinking stupidly. I watched his chest slowly deflate. Then he turned toward me and slowly shook his head. "Nice!" he hissed. "I need to talk to her."

I escorted Sinbad inside. He stopped when he saw a dozen packages piled on the kitchen table. It was all wild game carefully wrapped in white freezer paper, the contents identified by marker pen to include the species and date of kill. All appeared to be legal venison except one: inscribed with today's date, it contained the breast meat from the second turkey.

"Oh, Omar!" his wife cried. "These men think they found marijuana!" She had resigned herself to the fact that Sinbad was a poacher, but the idea of illegal drugs in her house seemed all but impossible.

Sinbad raised his palms defensively. "Whoa, honey. That's not Marijuana, it's just hay."

"Hay? What kind of hay?"

"I don't know . . . some kind of alfalfa that I found."

She shook her head wearily, her expression one of utter hopelessness. "Omar," she sighed. "What are you trying to do to me?"

She swooned suddenly. Sinbad quickly grabbed her and I pulled a chair from the kitchen table. "Ma'am. Please. Sit down."

Sinbad glanced at me; a flicker of gratitude crossed his face. Then he eased his wife into the chair and kneeled by her side. "You all right, baby?"

"Oh, Omar," she murmured. "What am I going to do with you?"

When I saw Barney's pickup truck backing into the driveway, I told Sinbad to step outside with Burchell and me. He squeezed his wife's shoulder and smiled at her. "Be right back." Then he followed us out the door.

Dobinick unlatched his tailgate and let it drop with a thud. He pulled two heavy wooden planks from the bed and ran them to the ground for a ramp. "Ready. Where's the ATV?"

"Around back," I said.

"Got the key?"

"That'd help, wouldn't it?" I turned to Sinbad and held out an open palm.

"Wait a minute. You're not taking my four-wheeler."

"Afraid so."

"What for?"

"It's evidence."

"I ain't giving you no key, and you ain't taking my quad!"

Fed up with Sinbad's attitude, I pulled out my handcuffs. "Look, mister, we're conducting a lawful investigation, and we have a search warrant. If you try to stop us from securing any evidence or continue to interfere, I'm going to shackle you and place you under arrest. Now hand me the key; I know you have one."

Sinbad stuffed both hands into his pockets and fished around for a moment. "I don't have it."

"Where is it?"

"I don't know—must have lost it."

"Have it your way," I said. "But the last person who wouldn't give me a key ended up with a damaged vehicle. We'll try not to bang up your machine too much getting it in the truck."

With that, Sinbad suddenly pivoted on his heels and bolted. I watched in stunned disbelief as he disappeared behind his trailer.

I took off after him. Within seconds I heard the staccato whine of an engine roaring to life. Suddenly his ATV came barreling around the corner in an astounding wheel-stand! Sinbad's red mane billowed wildly about his head, his lips were twisted in a lunatic grin.

Caught out in the open with no place to run, I braced myself for the massive impact raging toward me.

But in the flick of an eye, the awful machine swerved like a roller coaster glued to its track, and I felt a wicked blast of air as it passed within inches. I whipped around and watched it go straight for the truck, the front end dropping suddenly as it hit the ramp and launched upward, only to come to a bone-jarring stop in the truck's bed. Sinbad shut off the engine, then stood on the seat and leaped athletically to the ground. He walked over to the ramp, a smug grin on his face as he leaned back against the tailgate, arms folded tightly across his chest.

I walked up and held out my hand. "Key."

"I left it in the switch."

"That was a pretty reckless stunt."

He shrugged. "Just having some fun. Take care of my baby, man. I don't want to see any dents or scratches."

I lifted a plank and shoved it into the truck's bed. Sinbad watched me load the other one.

"When do I get it back?" he said.

I grabbed the tailgate and motioned with my chin for him to move. He slid off, and I rammed it shut. "You'll get your quad back when the case is settled. You can plead guilty or have a trial. Your choice."

Burchell, Dobinick, and I had nothing more to say to him. We got into our vehicles and drove off, leaving Sinbad standing alone in his driveway.

Later that year he pled guilty to killing two turkeys in closed season, paid a four-hundred dollar fine, and had his hunting license revoked for three years. He was also convicted of possessing marijuana. There was no jail sentence.

But it all meant little to Omar Sinbad. The following year, Burchell and I investigated a tip that he had killed a buck in closed season. Although there were witnesses, none dared testify against him, and we couldn't make a case.

We also received a number of anonymous tips about Sinbad hunting during his revocation period. The information always stale, the informants always nameless.

Years later, Sinbad moved into my district in Wyoming County where he remained a resident for the rest of my career. Although I received several complaints about his unlawful hunting during that time, none ever bore fruit. I did, however, manage to cross swords with his brother, Butch Striker, who made Omar seem like a choirboy in comparison. You can read about our wild encounter in my new book *Game Warden: Adventures of a Wildlife Warrior.*

Amos and Andy

THE NIGHT BORE a dismal, chilly mist as I drove through the quiet village at a snail's pace searching its sleepy streets. Acting on a tip from a voice on the phone, the thought loomed heavily that anonymous calls can turn out to be pranks. She had blurred her message quickly and hung up: *Amos Dudd just took a deer into his house. He lives in Mehoopany and has a red truck.* I had a name and a rural community in which to search. But without an actual street address, it began to look hopeless.

Dismayed after hours of searching, I had no sooner decided to head home when I spotted a red pickup truck parked next to a shabby looking house. Crammed into a dark driveway between two broken-down vehicles, I had almost missed it.

I stopped along the berm and parked. After calling the license tag into headquarters, I slid from my vehicle and walked through the dreary haze to the truck, a beat-up Dodge. The rear bumper, painted bright white, had a grapefruit-sized bloodstain on it like a big red bull's-eye. I shined my flashlight into the truck's bed where a clutter of flattened beer cans peeked out from under coiled snakes of steel cable and pieces of scrap lumber. In the far corner, a spare tire covered with thick cranberry-sauce clots of gore lay in plain view.

Stepping up to the truck's cab, I shined my flashlight through a side window. A Coleman spotlight lay face down on the seat along with a box of two-twenty-two hollow points. On the dashboard were two cartridge belts—one full, the other half empty. But the dashboard was covered with a thick film of dust while the gun belts were not, indicating they'd been recently used.

There was a thin line of blood trailing along the flagstone walkway toward the front of the house. I followed it to the glass storm door and peered into a well-lighted, empty mudroom. Here the blood trail continued across a worn linoleum floor and into a doorway leading to the main house. I banged on the glass and waited. Soon a bewhiskered, potbellied man stepped heavily into the room. He paused in brief alarm at my uniform before opening the door.

"State Game Commission," I said. "Are you Amos Dudd?"

His eyes flicked to his truck, then quickly back to me. "Yeah . . . ?"

"I'd like to talk to you about the blood in the back of your pickup."

"Oh, that!" he chuckled nervously. "It's just a roadkill I picked up tonight; that a problem?"

"Mind if I step in from the rain?"

He grinned at me with teeth black and broken. "Guess not," he said, opening the door.

I stepped into the mudroom and asked him for identification. Amos Dudd pulled out a wallet and handed me his driver's license. I wrote the information in my notebook and handed it back. "Where's the deer?"

Dudd shrugged. "It's gone. I threw it in the river. It was all mangled up; couldn't get much meat off it."

The Susquehanna River ran a hundred yards from Amos Dudd's house and had been boiling south at flood-stage for more than a week. "The deer should be halfway to the Chesapeake Bay by now," I remarked. "Guess you want me to take your word that it was a roadkill."

Dudd shook his head agreeably. "I think that would be the right thing to do."

I glanced at the floor. "Judging from all the blood, it looks like you brought the deer right through the house."

"I did. Come on, I'll show you."

I followed Dudd and what seemed a never-ending ribbon of blood as he shuffled into his kitchen. A teenage girl dressed in worn jeans and a faded cotton shirt sat at a wooden table and stared at us in a detached, weary sort of way. Scraps of raw venison, along with a cutting board and small boning knife, lay on the table in front of her.

Dudd continued through the room and paused by a door at the opposite end. He turned and grinned at me like a child sneaking into his parents' bedroom before opening it. I shadowed him into the adjoining space, a garage. Here the blood trail disappeared down a floor drain. From overhead, a large steel hook dangled on a heavy chain.

"See! There's no deer," Dudd said cheerily. Behind him, a rusty carpenter's saw, its jagged teeth choked with fleshy pulp and twisted strands of deer hair, lay on a windowsill of faded paint, peeling off in ugly, gnarled scabs.

It looked like Amos Dudd had disposed of the carcass. And if he tossed it into the river as he had said, it would be impossible to find. "Mind if I look in your freezer?"

"Nope. Look all you want." He turned and gestured me to follow with a broad wave of his hand. "Be my guest; you ain't gonna find nothing."

We walked into the kitchen, and he pointed toward a small adjoining room. "The freezer is in there."

I looked into the room. A battered upright freezer stood along the left wall, a stack of old newspapers and magazines piled on top. Several feet away, a man lay on his back in a rumpled cot. He looked up and grinned at me. "Come on in," he beckoned. "Want a drink?"

"I'm with the Pennsylvania Game Commission," I said, ignoring his comment.

"I know who you are," he assured me. He turned slowly and propped himself on an inebriated elbow. "Sure you don't want a drink, officer?" He was in his late fifties with a pudgy pink face and thinning snow-white hair that grew from the sides of his balding head and fell to his shoulders. A fierce beard sprouted from his face in every direction.

I opened the freezer door, surprised to find it well stocked with food but no venison. "What's your name, sir?" I asked.

"Andy," he said. "Andy Dudd."

"Is this your house?"

"Nope! My son, Amos, pays the rent. Something wrong, officer (sounded like ossifer)?"

"Your son brought a deer into the house tonight. Where is it?"

"Don't ask me!" he snorted. "I've been lying here all night—drunk! Want to look under my bed?"

"And if I did, what would I find?"

Andy Dudd belched vociferously. "Nothing! But you're welcome to look. Go ahead, look anywhere you want. You ain't gonna find no deer."

And of course, he was right. The deer was long gone. I suspected that Amos Dudd's wife had made off with the venison before I could get there. I walked back into the kitchen. "You obviously got some meat off the deer before disposing of it. Where is it?"

"I ate it!" said Dudd.

"All of it?"

"Yep. I told you, I didn't get much." He brushed a thick straggle of hair from his face and eyed me warily. Dudd knew that I suspected the deer was no roadkill and that he had shot it, but he didn't much care. All that mattered was what I could prove. And he was certain that without a deer, I couldn't make a case against him.

"Do you own any guns?" I asked.

"Yeah, I own a few."

"Mind if I look at them?"

"They're upstairs." He nodded suggestively. "Come on, I'll show you."

As I followed Dudd up a long wooden staircase, slick, portly roaches flashed under our feet. But a few dallied, and Amos Dudd's jaded boots eagerly crushed them as he climbed, leaving their ruptured bodies lying in his wake.

He led me down a narrow hallway littered with unwashed clothes and children's broken toys until we reached a bedroom at the far end. A rumpled bed stood by the left wall, a woman's flannel bathrobe carelessly tossed upon it in a loose pile. Dirty clothes were strewn everywhere, and in a small alcove a child's mattress lay on the wood floor.

"Who sleeps there?" I asked.

"One of my kids."

"How many do you have?"

"Four."

"Where are they?"

"They left with my wife to see her dad, why?"

"Just curious." A feeling of utter disgust washed over me knowing that his children lived in such squalor.

Dudd opened a closet door and reached inside. I quickly unsnapped my revolver. "Easy," I said. "I'll get the guns."

He stepped aside as I retrieved five cased firearms from the closet and laid them on the rumpled bed. I checked the caliber of each one. "Do you own a two-twenty-two?"

"Nope!"

"Then why do you have those caliber bullets in your truck?"

"My dad has one. They're *his* bullets."

"Where's his rifle?"

"It ain't here," Dudd said with a feral grin. "He knows he'd never get it back if it was. He keeps it at his place."

Like father, like son, I figured. I went back downstairs with Amos Dudd and started gathering the venison scraps from his kitchen table. I pulled a plastic sandwich bag from my coat pocket and dropped the meat inside.

Dudd scratched his shaggy head and wrinkled a thick brow. "Hungry?" he chuckled sarcastically.

"Evidence," I said. "By the way, if this is a roadkilled deer, guess you won't mind telling me where you found it."

"No, I don't mind at all. It was up the road apiece."

"Want to show me? There should be some blood or skid marks—maybe even some broken glass or pieces of plastic to back up your story."

Dudd fixed his gaze on the ceiling, eyelids fluttering wildly. "Well now, let's see . . . as I recall, the deer wasn't actually on the road. It was in a field. My dad and I were spotlighting when we saw it. There might've been some blood, but with this rain you probably won't find any now."

Tired of the charade, I could feel my jaw set. "Mr. Dudd, I don't believe you picked up a roadkill. I think you and your father shot the deer. Your story is too convenient and too full of holes: you threw the deer in the river; you ate all the meat—I don't believe any of it!

"I'm going to file charges against both you and your father for possessing a deer killed in closed season. You can each either plead guilty or tell your story to the judge."

Dudd thought for a few seconds and then nodded his head with firm conviction. "Tell you what: I believe in our judicial system. I'll take a trial."

I stepped outside, glad to get away from the man, and began taking photographs of the bloody pickup truck. The rain had let up, and I could see a sky full of bright, twinkling stars. It had been a long night, and dawn would soon be breaking. With it would come another long day of patrol, as Pennsylvania's small game season was already in full swing.

Later that week I filed a charges against Amos and Andy Dudd. They took hearings before the judge and were found guilty of unlawfully possessing a deer in closed season, the father fined five hundred dollars, his son a thousand.

Pennsylvania law excludes deer alleged as roadkills for a defense in judicial proceedings. Otherwise, poachers could shoot deer all season long and claim they found the carcasses along the road. Of course, if a suspect can show that his deer was indeed killed along a highway, the decision whether to prosecute or not is left up to the officer's discretion.

I reported Amos Dudd to the Department of Child Welfare, requesting they look into the living conditions his children were forced to endure. A few months later, Amos Dudd's house was vacated. I never ran into him or his father again.

Two Men and a Truck

HIS JEEP CONCEALED in moon shadow at the road's edge, the deputy observed the dark valley below. There had been a report of shots fired less than an hour ago—two in rapid succession from a high-powered rifle. And as he watched from his vantage point high atop a tall ridge, a spotlight began its sweep across the fields below him. He grabbed his binoculars off the dashboard and peered into them. Three deer stood like statues in a grassy meadow, the spotlight captivating them in its powerful beam.

He focused on a knoll seventy yards from the deer. A pickup truck was stopped along the road, the light streaming from an open window like a laser. He saw the passenger's door creep open, the interior lamp revealing two silhouettes. The one at the door slipped out with a rifle in his hands. The other held the spotlight.

The deputy zeroed in on the poacher as he crouched low, using the truck to shield himself from the unsuspecting deer. Reaching the front fender, he slowly raised his body and leaned over the hood with his gun. The three deer paid him no mind as they grazed on tender grasses in preparation for the coming winter.

The man in the truck kept his light on the biggest animal, a robust eight-point buck, as his partner braced himself for a clean shot.

The deputy could have activated his red lights or blasted his siren and perhaps save the deer, but that would've only made the poachers flee. Their vehicle was well ahead of him. He'd have to give chase along a narrow township road, and he didn't want to risk an accident with another vehicle. It wasn't worth it. Better to let them take the deer, he thought, then move in while they were dragging the heavy carcass back toward the road.

Suddenly the one holding the spotlight let out a thunderous sneeze—so explosive, it was, that the deputy could hear it from afar. Alerted to the impending danger, the deer lifted their heads in unison. They froze for only a second, noses pointed toward the truck, then turned to bolt into the surrounding woods with their white tails held high.

The deputy turned his ignition key and brought his vehicle to life. He decked the accelerator, swallowing the distance between them. He came upon a dirt lane that cut through a field to his right: Wildcat Road. It would lead him to the poachers. He cut his wheels and raced down the narrow lane, hoping to block their escape. Suddenly three deer bolted across the road in front of him—the same deer that had fled from the poacher's light. He slammed the brake, skidding sideways, almost rolling his Jeep before coming to a jarring stop perpendicular to the lane, blocking it.

He shook the cobwebs out of his head and looked toward the knoll where the poachers had been. Through the gloom he saw the dim outline of their vehicle. It was coming straight at him with its headlights off.

The deputy quickly exited his Jeep, his uniform incandescent in the glow of red emergency lights as he raised a hand, signaling the truck to halt.

The truck slammed to a stop, tires digging into the gravel, only a few yards separating him from its wheels. Then the headlights flashed on, temporarily blinding him, and the truck began to inch forward.

The deputy bravely stood his ground, palm on the butt of his revolver. Would they mow him down over a deer? It seemed impossible.

In a breath the truck's front bumper was gnawing at his leg, the pulsing chug of its motor like a panting in his brain. There was no time to think. Acting on pure instinct, he placed a knee on the bumper and leaped on the hood, bracing himself so he wouldn't fall under the crushing wheels. He could see two men inside, two rifles on the seat between them. And in that fleeting second he realized he was outnumbered and outgunned. Reaching back with his right hand, he pulled a heavy-barreled revolver from his holster and leveled it at the driver.

The truck slammed to a shuddering stop, and the deputy jumped off. He stood with his gun pointed into their open window. "Put your hands on the dashboard, right now!"

Both men stared back at him with stony faces. He knew they had guns. One could be pointed in his face at any second. In a flash of motion he jerked open the door and grabbed the driver, forcing him out with a painful wristlock.

There was no time to frisk him for weapons; the other man had access to the rifles. Using the first poacher for cover, he jerked his wrist hard, sending him to his toes as he sidestepped behind him. "Tell your friend to get out or I'll break it!"

"Ahhh! Sammy, do what he says!"

The other slid across the seat and got out. He stood by the open door with his hands in the air.

"Move to the front of the truck!" ordered the deputy. He released the first man's wrist and shoved him toward his companion. "You too!"

He went to the truck and switched off the ignition, dropping the keys into his coat pocket. Breathing in measured beats to ease his racing heart, he detached a portable radio from his belt and called for backup.

Both poachers stood by the truck as he reported his location to the dispatcher. He saw the one with the sore wrist mouth something to his companion. The other nodded back, and they came at him.

The driver was first, his eyes locked in a cold glare as he lunged. The deputy drew a baton from a ring on his belt and drove the tip into his gut. His attacker heaved a croaking gasp and doubled over, clutching his stomach with both hands. Then he dropped to his knees and retched. The other man stopped dead in his tracks and stared at his companion, drool spilling in a stream from his lips. When he looked up he saw the deputy's hand on his revolver, and he began to back away.

Satisfied they'd stay put for a while, the deputy climbed into the cab of their truck. Along with their rifles he found a shotgun, several boxes of ammunition, four knives, and a spotlight. He carted the weapons to his Jeep and locked them inside. Both men glared at him as he walked back to their vehicle and dropped the tailgate. He shined his flashlight into the bed. It was covered with fresh blood.

When the call came over my radio that a deputy needed help, I pushed my engine to its limit. It was late. Traffic almost nonexistent. The only thing I had to worry about was a deer jumping in front of me. Ironic, when I considered it.

I raced full bore down Highway Six, white passing stripes becoming a solid line on the macadam, red lights arcing into a coal-black sky. I knew what it was like to confront hostile poachers in the dead of night without backup. It took nerves of steel. The suspects were always armed, and often strung out on booze or drugs. Sometimes both. Many have extensive criminal records. A history of violence. Anything could happen. And as I rocketed down the highway, my greatest fear was that I would be too late, that some terrible thing would happen before I could prevent it. I felt my hands tighten on the steering wheel. A dull, throbbing pain began to grow in the back of my head. I glanced at the speedometer. The needle buried. In five more minutes I'd be there.

When I turned into Wildcat Road, I spotted my deputy's Jeep stopped at a wild angle. Thinking the worst, I pulled close and saw a Dodge Ram stopped opposite his Jeep. Two men stood by the truck, my deputy guarding them.

I leaped from my vehicle and hustled over. "Are you okay?"

"I'm fine," said the deputy. "It got a little hairy for a moment, but we understand each other now."

"Thank God," I said. "Have they been searched?"

"Be my guest. I'll cover you."

I had both men face their truck and lean into it with their palms outstretched, feet spread wide. I patted them down. Although they had no concealed weapons, both men had wallets. I took them and pulled out their motor vehicle licenses. The driver's name was Aldo Beretta, his buddy, Samuel Ryno. They were sixty miles from their homes in the Pocono Mountains. There was plenty of good hunting out that way, I thought. Why come all the way out here to kill a deer? They must have had friends or relatives somewhere close by.

As my deputy briefed me about his dangerous ride on the hood of their truck, my mood darkened. The two men standing quietly before us were not your average blockheads looking to jacklight a deer. Not only did they have a reckless disregard for the law, their foolish antics could have severely injured or even killed my deputy.

"I want to show you something," he said. I followed him to the truck and watched him shine his flashlight into the bed. A large bloodstain mixed with deer hair lay in the center of it. Fresh deer droppings were scattered about too, and even more blood could be seen on the tailgate and bumper.

"What do you think the temperature is right now?" he asked.

"Low teens," I said. "Never got above freezing all day."

He pressed a fingertip into some blood and held it in front of me. A crimson stain against his skin. "Still tacky. In this weather the blood would have frozen solid in less than an hour."

I nodded. "They must have just killed one and hidden the carcass somewhere."

"I wonder how many more they would have shot if I hadn't stopped them?"

"Good question," I said. "They probably have a place to store the carcasses close by. I'll see if I can get them to talk."

I started with Samuel Ryno. A stout five-feet-eight with broad shoulders and a muscular neck, his deeply tanned face bore a dense mustache that grew in a perpetual frown, giving him the gruff appearance of a hired gun from the old west.

"I want to ask you some questions," I said.

He rolled his eyes at me and looked away. "You're wasting your time."

"Maybe. Let's walk to the back of the truck."

I shined my flashlight on the blood and hair in the bed so he could see it. "You had a deer in your truck. Where is it?"

Ryno shrugged. "I don't know what you're talking about."

"There's blood and hair all over your vehicle. What happened to the carcass?"

He stuffed his hands in his pockets and stared at me.

"And the blood on your boots?"

He glanced down at them. "I don't know how it got there."

It was obvious he'd been around the block a few times; he had an attitude you could almost touch. He was convinced that as long as we didn't have a dead deer we didn't have a case. "Last chance," I offered. "Or else we'll do this the hard way."

"Cop talk," he sneered. "You don't scare me."

I escorted Ryno back to the front of the truck and had him place his hands on the hood. Hoping for better luck with Beretta, I motioned him to the tailgate.

Beretta shuffled back, then faced me with deep-set eyes that were almost feral. Tall and lanky with shoulder-length hair, his hollowed cheeks and pale skin gave him the gaunt look of a drug addict. The physical contradiction of his companion.

"What happened to the deer that was in your truck?"

Beretta folded his arms across his chest and shrugged. "I didn't have a deer in my truck."

I shined the bed with my light. "Then where did all the blood come from?"

He said nothing. His eyes fixing on me like two burning coals.

"You might want to cooperate," I said. "It's cold out tonight. The Poconos are a long way off."

"What are you getting at?"

"Truck looks brand new. Is it yours?"

A stiff nod.

"All blood looks alike," I said. "For all I know, it could be human."

"It's not human, man. Get real."

"Well, if it's not from a human or a deer, what did it come from?"

Beretta shrugged. "I got nothing else to say."

I stopped asking questions. After all, my deputy had watched both men attempting to kill a deer with a light. That alone would carry a thousand dollar fine for each of them. And because deer season was closed, the fresh blood and hair in their truck would be enough to charge them with the possession of an illegal deer. Although an admission of guilt would have been helpful, it wasn't essential in order to move forward with an arrest. "Go on back and stand with your buddy," I said. "We're finished."

Beretta turned to walk away, then he spun around and came at me, his face frozen in a lunatic gaze. I was ready for him. I drove two fists into his chest, pivoting on my heels while simultaneously rotating my hips to emphasize the blow. The impact lifted him off the ground and sent him crashing into the side of his truck. He stood there for a moment in stunned silence. Then his knees buckled and he dropped on them, boney arms clasping his chest as he expelled a long, convulsive sob.

My deputy had been watching. He smiled and shook his head in wonder. "Some guys never learn."

I walked back to my patrol car and radioed for a wrecker. Beretta pulled himself up painfully and shuffled close to Ryno. And in a low voice, I overheard him speak: "Sammy, why don't we just tell 'em it was a roadkill and get this over with?"

Pretending not to hear, I pulled a camera from my coat pocket and began snapping pictures of the truck's bed, thinking that if they wanted to claim that the blood came from a roadkill, it would at least be a start—a sign that they might want to talk, make some kind of a deal perhaps.

I spent a half hour or so collecting blood scrapings, hair samples, and other evidence from the truck. Then, after attaching seizure tags to the firearms and the other gear discovered by my deputy, I approached both men once again and asked about the deer that had been in their vehicle.

Beretta, still brooding from our encounter, rubbed his chest nervously. "What if I tell you it was a—"

Ryno cut him off. "Shut up!" he barked. Then he turned to me. "You're never gonna find it. And without a deer you can't prove a thing!"

Suddenly the throaty rumble of a heavy vehicle began to roll toward us, its elevated headlights slicing through the darkness as it made its way slowly down Wildcat Road. The poachers watched with keen interest as the big wrecker backed up to their truck and positioned itself a few feet from the bumper before stopping.

"Hey, Bill!" the driver called cheerily. He jumped from the cab and nodded toward the pickup. "This the one?"

"Sorry to drag you out so late, Curt," I called back. "Yes, go ahead and load it."

Beretta and Ryno stared in silent gloom as he snapped a heavy chain under pickup's chassis and walked to the front of his rig. Curt pushed a button on the wrecker's frame, and a powerful motor thrummed as their truck was hoisted upon the rig's tilted platform

"You can't do this!" Beretta howled. *"That's a twenty thousand dollar truck!"*

Curt ignored Beretta's protest as he checked to make sure the pickup had been loaded securely. Then he climbed into his rig, dropped it into gear, and disappeared into the night.

"I can't believe you took my truck!" moaned Beretta. "What do you want from me?"

"Nothing," I said. "You're both free to go."

"Go where? We don't have a truck!"

I turned and walked toward my patrol car. The night was growing colder by the minute. "You'll both be receiving citations in the mail," I said over my shoulder. "Have a nice walk."

Both men stared at me in disbelief. And for a moment, I thought they might talk. Instead, they turned and began walking toward the distant highway. I was certain they knew someone close by. Someone they wanted to protect. The deer would be there, too. In a secret place. A place I never found.

Aldo Beretta and Samuel Ryno were charged with eleven separate Game Law violations. Months later, in district court, both men showed up with attorneys.

In preparation, I had the hair and blood evidence from their truck analyzed by the State Police Crime Lab. I needed scientific proof to back up my charge, as the defense attorneys were sure to challenge this.

In court, I presented Crime Lab reports showing that the blood and hair taken from Beretta's truck indeed came from a whitetail deer. I stated further that although deer season didn't open until the following morning, the blood was fresh and wet; therefore, it had to come from a deer that had been killed within hours. When I finished testifying, my deputy took the stand and testified about the deer the two men had attempted to kill with a rifle and a light. Additionally, our combined testimony about their reckless and aggressive behavior didn't set well with the judge at all. When the dust cleared, they were convicted on all charges and sentenced to pay more than four-thousand dollars in fines. In addition, both men had their hunting and trapping privileges revoked. Samuel Ryno received four years revocation, Aldo Beretta five more, for a total of nine.

Ryno paid off his fine within a matter of weeks, but Beretta was much slower. He had requested monthly payments. The judge had graciously agreed. But his checks started coming in later each month. Eventually he stopped sending payments altogether, and a warrant was issued for his arrest.

Monroe County Game Warden, Dean Beach, picked up Beretta at his job and transported him back to Wyoming County where he turned him over to me. I was surprised to see that Beretta had trimmed his hair stylishly short. His color looked better too. But his eyes bore the same detached, icy look they had the night I arrested him.

I hauled him into District Court. Judge Patricia Robinson reminded him that he had failed to make a payment in over three months and gave him an opportunity to make a phone call before committing him to the county jail.

I walked him to a phone just outside the court. He dialed a number and listened to it ring several times before someone picked up. "Honey, it's me," he moaned. "You gotta help me. I'm going to jail."

There was a fretful murmuring on the other end.

Berretta quickly cut in. "—I thought *you* were paying it!"

The voice got louder, confrontational. Berretta promptly backed off. "No-no-no," he pleaded. "Don't hang up! I'm sorry. My fault. Look . . . just come for me. Bring money, too. Okay?

Click . . . !

I escorted Aldo Beretta to the county jail in handcuffs. A modern facility only several years old, it was painted a brilliant white. And from the outside, one would hardly know it was a jail at all—the only hint being a conspicuous absence of windows. A handsome landscape of flowering shrubbery hugged the beguiling prison walls as I ushered him from the back parking lot to a heavy steel door and pushed the buzzer.

"Yes?" came a voice though a speaker above us. It was female.

"State game warden with a prisoner."

A loud metallic clank told us the formidable door had been unlocked. I stepped into a small chamber of concrete walls with my shackled prisoner. The door closed with a hollow thud. Removing my handgun from my holster, I placed it into a steel gun safe recessed into the wall. I closed the safe's door, locked it, and dropped the key into my pocket. A jail guard watched me do this from a bulletproof window before unlatching a second heavy door.

Aldo Beretta and I stepped into the sterile chamber where all new prisoners are inaugurated. I removed his handcuffs and handed the commitment paper to one of two male guards. He looked it over and glanced impassively at Beretta. "You're in luck," he said. "We only have one bed left."

"I'm not staying overnight!" protested Beretta in a voice edged with dread. "My wife's on her way over here with the money."

The guard shrugged indifferently. "That may be, but this paper says you're staying right here until we get word from the judge."

"But wait a minute!—"

"We even have lunch for you if we get done in time."

"Done?" Beretta yelped. "Done *what?*"

The guard pursed his lips, cocked an eyebrow, and nodded toward his companion. "First we gotta do a thorough search."

I watched Beretta's face turn ghostly white, and for a moment, thought the idea of eating prison food might have triggered a sense of nausea. But as I turned to leave, I saw a second guard standing grimly by an interior doorway. He had just finished snapping on a fresh pair of latex gloves.